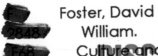

*Culture and
Customs of
Argentina*

Culture and Customs of Argentina

David William Foster
Melissa Fitch Lockhart
Darrell B. Lockhart

Culture and Customs of Latin America
and the Caribbean
Peter Standish, Series Editor

GREENWOOD PRESS
Westport, Connecticut • London

Library of Congress Cataloging-in-Publication Data

Foster, David William.
    Culture and customs of Argentina / David William Foster, Melissa
Fitch Lockhart, Darrell B. Lockhart.
        p.   cm.—(Culture and customs of Latin America and the
Caribbean, ISSN 1521–8856)
    Includes bibliographical references and index.
    ISBN 0–313–30319–3 (alk. paper)
    1. Argentina—Civilization—20th century.   2. Argentina—Social
life and customs.   I. Lockhart, Melissa Fitch.   II. Lockhart,
Darrell B.   III. Title.   IV. Series.
    F2848.F68   1998
    982.06—dc21   98–15325

British Library Cataloguing in Publication Data is available.

Library of Congress Catalog Card Number: 98–15325
ISBN: 0–313–30319–3
ISSN: 1521–8856

First published in 1998

Greenwood Press, 88 Post Road West, Westport, CT 06881
An imprint of Greenwood Publishing Group, Inc.

Printed in the United States of America

The paper used in this book complies with the
Permanent Paper Standard issued by the National
Information Standards Organization (Z39.48–1984).

10 9 8 7 6 5 4 3 2

Contents

Illustrations

Series Foreword

"CULTURE" is a problematic word. In everyday language we tend to use it in at least two senses. On the one hand we speak of cultured people and places full of culture, uses that imply a knowledge or presence of certain forms of behavior or of artistic expression that are socially prestigious. In this sense large cities and prosperous people tend to be seen as the most cultured. On the other hand, there is an interpretation of "culture" that is broader and more anthropological; culture in this broader sense refers to whatever traditions, beliefs, customs, and creative activities characterize a given community—in short, it refers to what makes that community different from others. In this second sense, everyone has culture; indeed, it is impossible to be without culture.

The problems associated with the idea of culture have been exacerbated in recent years by two trends: less respectful use of language and a greater blurring of cultural differences. Nowadays, "culture" often means little more than behavior, attitude, or atmosphere. We hear about the culture of the boardroom, of the football team, of the marketplace; there are books with titles like *The Culture of War* by Richard Gabriel (Greenwood, 1990) or *The Culture of Narcissism* by Christopher Lasch (1979). In fact, as Christopher Clausen points out in a recent article published in the *American Scholar* (Summer 1996), we have gotten ourselves into trouble by using the term so sloppily.

People who study culture generally assume that culture (in the anthropological sense) is learned, not genetically determined. Another general assumption made in these days of multiculturalism has been that cultural differences should be respected rather than put under pressure to change. But these assumptions, too, have sometimes proved to be problematic. For instance, multiculturalism is a fine ideal, but in practice it is not always easy to reconcile with the beliefs of the very people who advocate it: for example, is female circumcision an issue of human rights or just a different cultural practice?

The blurring of cultural differences is a process that began with the steamship, increased with radio, and is now racing ahead with the Internet. We are becoming globally homogenized. Since the English-speaking world (and the United States in particular) is the dominant force behind this process of homogenization, it behooves us to make efforts to understand the sensibilities of members of other cultures.

This series of books, a contribution toward that greater understanding, deals with the neighbors of the United States, with people who have just as much right to call themselves Americans. What are the historical, institutional, religious, and artistic features that make up the modern culture of such peoples as the Haitians, the Chileans, the Jamaicans, and the Guatemalans? How are their habits and assumptions different from our own? What can we learn from them? As we familiarize ourselves with the ways of other countries, we come to see our own from a new perspective.

Each volume in the series focuses on a single country. With slight variations to accommodate national differences, each begins by outlining the historical, political, ethnic, geographical, and linguistic context, as well as the religious and social customs, and then proceeds to a discussion of a variety of artistic activities, including the press, the media, the cinema, music, literature, and the visual and performing arts. The authors are all intimately acquainted with the countries concerned: some were born or brought up in them, and each has a professional commitment to enhancing the understanding of the culture in question.

We are inclined to suppose that our ways of thinking and behaving are normal. And so they are . . . for us. We all need to realize that ours is only one culture among many, and that it is hard to establish by any rational criteria that ours as a whole is any better (or worse) than any other. As individual members of our immediate community, we know that we must learn to respect our differences from one another. Respect for differences between cultures is no less vital. This is particularly true of the United States, a nation of immigrants, but one that sometimes seems to be bent on destroying variety at home, and, worse still, on having others follow suit. By learning about other people's cultures, we come to understand and respect them; we earn their respect for us; and, not least, we see ourselves in a new light.

Peter Standish
East Carolina University

Introduction

TO BE SURE, all of the countries of Latin America have unique and fascinating histories. Argentina, however, is one of the few countries that holds a special "continental" interest (continental referring to Latin America as a whole). Of all of the Latin American countries, it went from being one of the absolute backwaters of the Spanish Empire to one of the wealthiest, most dynamic modern societies. The twentieth century has seen major political and economic problems that have given rise to successive military tyrannies and elected governments of questionable constitutional democracy; nevertheless, at the present moment Argentina is, without a doubt, a leader among Latin American nations. It is one that the U.S. government has accorded a favored nation status (a status granted by the U.S. government to close allies with specific economic, tariff, and immigration provisions) and one that has every intention of being a major player on the international scene. Indeed, in recent years, Argentina has vied energetically for a permanent seat on the United Nations Security Council (Brazil has similar interests, as Latin America's largest nation; others have proposed a rotating Latin American seat).

Argentina "dollarized" its economy in the early 1990s, and the result has been a firm—if for many not untroubled—niche in the contemporary free-market growth system that has brought currency stability to that country and a large number of trading partnerships with the United States and other major industrial societies. While Brazil and Chile have also gone the same route (Mexico has had serious setbacks in a similar undertaking), it is in Argentina where one finds a well-established middle class, a high level of buying power in the hands of a fairly broad (by Latin American societies)

An *olla popular* (people's kettle), the soup kitchens that have fed the poor in outlying areas of the city and in the province of Buenos Aires since both the economic devastations wrought by the military dictatorships and the impoverishment created by neoliberal economic policies of democratic governments. Courtesy of Eduardo Gil.

spectrum of citizens, and a standard of living that is, at least in the central core areas of Buenos Aires and other major cities, the envy of Latin America.

Argentina's current prosperity is only the latest stage in a series of cycles that, although they may have at times brought serious economic setbacks and political disasters, have given the country a unique place in Latin American society. As a country that tends to be defined in terms of its capital, the major port city of Buenos Aires, where one third of the population of the nation is concentrated (another third is concentrated along the river system that stretches north and northwest from Buenos Aires), Argentina has long looked toward Europe and now toward the United States for many aspects of its identity. One tends to associate with Argentina the most excessive effects of rapid modernization, which has caused profound sociopolitical divisions. Society, in its attempt to come to terms with the tensions, ambiguities, and international contradictions of this modernization, has often fostered divisions between Buenos Aires and the rest of the nation. But if there is any credence in the proposition that cultural production exists in a proportional relationship to the extent of conflicts within a society, Argentina would certainly provide ample supporting evidence.

The present volume is an introduction to what is significantly unique about Argentine society. American readers tend to have a homogeneous (if highly fragmented and uneven) image of Latin America as a single society. Certainly, there are similarities among the Latin American nations, however some features of Argentine history contribute to Argentina's unique national profile. Argentina defines itself in terms of Buenos Aires, the largest port city in the region. It is also overwhelmingly an immigrant society (Buenos Aires has the largest Jewish population in Latin America and one of the largest in the world). Argentina has always been a cultural innovator; it is home to the tango, writer Jorge Luis Borges, theater, a film industry, and book and magazine publishing. Finally, extreme dimensions of its political history (the Peronista experiment, neofascist military dictatorships, and current authoritarian democracy) have added to the uniqueness of Argentina.

The chapters that make up this volume suggest what makes Argentina socially and culturally interesting and highlight what aspects of its society may be of interest to American readers.

Chronology

1536   The Pedro de Mendoza expedition landed in the Río de la Plata and founded Buenos Aires. This was not a permanent settlement. Misunderstandings between the Spaniards and the Indians resulted in attacks, lack of food, and suffering for the expedition. Mendoza, seriously ill, returned to Spain.

1542–1544   The Diego de Rojas expedition advanced from Perú into northwest Argentina and founded the first towns of Salta and Tucumán. The Spaniards established *encomiendas* (trusts) with the native population. In 1573 Governor Jerónimo Luis de Cabrera founded Córdoba del Tucumán in a site that would provide future trade routes between Río de la Plata and Upper Perú.

1580   Juan de Garay founded Buenos Aires a second time. In 1620 there were 212 Spanish householders in the town. Buenos Aires was ruled by a governor who depended on Upper Perú Viceroyalties. The excellent port city, as well as a weak administrative organization, gave Buenos Aires the reputation of providing opportunities for contraband.

1776   Carlos III of Spain created the Viceroyalty of the Río de la Plata with eight intendancies: Buenos Aires, Córdoba, Salta, Potosí, Charcas, La Paz, and Paraguay. The viceroy, appointed directly by the crown, centralized the administration of justice and military command. The geographical divisions of the intendancy system in Río de la Plata were the basis of the future nations of Argentina, Uruguay, Paraguay, and Bolivia. The major economic activity during the eighteenth century was ranching. Buenos Aires gradually became an export port and financial capital.

1806   British Admiral Sir Home Popham and General William Beresford captured Buenos Aires. A largely Creole militia, under Santiago de Liniers, drove them out of the city. One year later, there was a new British attack on Buenos Aires with the same result.

1810   The decline of Spain in the conflict with Napoléon accelerated the demands for the establishment of the *Primera Junta* (First Ruling Junta) on May 25 in Buenos Aires, independent from the Spaniards.

1816   In the provincial town of San Miguel de Tucumán, a congress of representatives from the whole country declared formal independence on July 9.

1817   An army, under the liberator General José de San Martín, crossed the Andes into Chile to begin a series of campaigns against the Spanish forces. The Army of the Andes successfully assured freedom to Chile and Perú.

1826   Bernardino Rivadavia became first president of Argentina under the terms of a centralist constitution produced by Buenos Aires.

1829   A wealthy rancher and exporter of salt beef, Juan Manuel de Rosas assumed the governorship of Buenos Aires Province with dictatorial powers until 1852. Although Rosas attacked the Unitario party's centralist agenda and supported Federalist principles, his effective defense of the ranchers' interests and cattle exportation reinforced the leadership of Buenos Aires.

1833   The British navy took the Falkland Islands, or Islas Malvinas, by force.

1852	In February, Rosas's forces were defeated in the battle of Caseros by General Justo José de Urquiza, strong man of Entre Ríos Province. Rosas fled to England, where he lived as an exile.
1853	Under the auspices of Urquiza, a constituent convention wrote the Argentine constitution with a federalist structure but conferred extensive powers on national authorities.
1865	Argentina, with Brazil and Uruguay, was involved in the war of the Triple Alliance against Paraguay until 1870.
1868	The leader of public education, Domingo Faustino Sarmiento, became president. The government was able to move its military forces against natives across a growing rail network.
1880	Under the presidency of General Julio A. Roca, Buenos Aires was formally declared a federal district. Patagonia was incorporated into the national territory through the Conquest of the Desert, directed by Roca against the still autonomous Indian tribes. Immigration increased, particularly of Spaniards, Italians, and Jews. Argentina had at this time political unity and growing ties with the international market.
1916	By universal vote, Hipólito Yrigoyen of the Radical party was chosen president; he was the first popular leader in South America.
1930	Commanded by General José Félix Uriburu, on September 6, the first antidemocratic military revolution in Argentina took place against Yrigoyen's second presidency.
1946	The emergence of Juan Domingo Perón divided the country between traditional parties and Peronists. In his two periods of government, Perón maintained the power on the basis of the relationship between union movements and his own political movement.
1952	Evita Perón, the charismatic wife of the president, who had obtained the vote for women and championed social programs, died. Her death was a serious blow to the for-

tunes of the government. Her state funeral inaugurated a continuing legacy of Evita as a legendary national figure.

1955   Military forces led a coup against an increasingly dictatorial and politically impoverished Perón government. The death of Eva Perón in 1952, idol of millions of working-class Argentines, had accelerated the collapse of the regime. Perón went into exile. For many years he lived in Madrid.

1973   After decades of military interventions in the country's democratic life, President General Alejandro A. Lanusse was forced by political agitation, strikes, and guerrilla action to call elections with the participation of the banned Peronista party. On May 25 the Peronist candidate, Héctor J. Cámpora, assumed office as president; however, three months later, he resigned and through new elections Perón returned to power once again. Perón's third presidency ended with his death on July 4, 1974.

1976   The succession by Isabel Perón, Perón's third wife and vice-president, to the presidency was accompanied by economic problems, institutional disorder, and violent terrorism activities. On March 26 the military returned to power and overthrew her government with popular support. Nevertheless, the new junta not only destroyed the urban guerrilla movement, but engaged in a dirty war against political dissidence that resulted in the disappearance of thousands of persons, many now known to be innocent of any crime.

1982   President General Leopoldo Galtieri decided on April 2 to invade the British-held Falklands (Islas Malvinas). By June the Royal Marines and the British Army had retaken the islands, and the humiliation of Argentine military government was complete.

1983   With the election of Raúl Alfonsín from the Radical party as president, Argentina returned to democracy. Alfonsín sponsored the Permanent Assembly for Human Rights, which judged the military crimes during the "dirty war."

1989	Unchecked inflation led to a tumultuous end of Alfonsín's presidency. He turned the government over early to president-elect Carlos Saúl Menem. Argentina began a new political era marked by political compromise with the past and efforts to stimulate neoliberal development and foreign investment.
1990	Menem dollarized the Argentine economy and signed the *Ley de Punto final* (Final point law) to put an end to judgments against military leaders responsible for tyranny and human rights abuses. The Argentine navy formed part of the international peace force during the Persian Gulf War.
1994	Menem won a second presidency. Argentina became part of the Mercosur with Brazil and Chile. However, the stabilization of the peso has not allowed Argentina to emerge yet from bankruptcy.

1

Context

THE PURPOSE OF this chapter is to establish some contextual bases to help the reader understand Argentine history, society, and cultural production. It is not a chronological enumeration—a chronology is included in the previous chapter—and although the following section on history describes major events and individuals, the purpose of this chapter is to identify major conceptual elements. These elements include the role of Argentina among Latin American countries, the sociocultural issues that make up what can be called a national self-consciousness or identity, and the most salient political phenomena that are traditionally identified with Argentina, both from the point of view of that nation and from the point of view of other nations.

HISTORY

Argentina is one of the Latin American republics that resulted from the breakup of the Spanish colonial empire in the Americas in the early nineteenth century. The movement for independence, led by Creole merchants and assisted by rebel irregulars in rural areas, brought about Argentina's separation from Spain. This separation came about in two stages: (1) On May 25, 1810, leaders of Buenos Aires repudiated their allegiance to the Spanish crown following Napoleon's French invasion of the peninsula; they did, however, affirm their allegiance to the Spanish king; (2) On July 9, 1816, independence was declared; it would not be until 1853, after internal wars, that the republic would be declared. Argentina embarked on a period of almost fifty years of rivalry that established the primacy of the city of

Buenos Aires and the preeminence of the urban mercantile class in concert with the landed oligarchic government, with beef exporting as the principal economic activity. By the latter quarter of the nineteenth century, Argentina had already begun to emerge as a South American superpower, exercising considerable economic, political, social, and cultural influence throughout the continent.

Although much of what today is Argentina was originally settled by individuals who emigrated from colonial populations in the north, the focal point of settlement has long been the city of Buenos Aires, today the second largest city in the Southern Hemisphere and the third largest city in Latin America (after Mexico City and São Paulo). Spanish settlers originally came ashore in the Río de la Plata estuary in 1535; however, the settlement did not prosper. The lack of sources of wealth as they were then defined by the Spaniards and the hostility of the essentially nomadic indigenous people forced the Spaniards to move inland and northward, toward what is today Asunción. In their retreat, horses brought by the Spaniards were left loose on the Pampas, and the combination of superb grazing and mild temperatures soon provided the plains with the herds of mustangs that became legendary. Juan de Garay founded Buenos Aires for a second time in 1580. This time, the settlement took hold, as Buenos Aires became important to the active pirate trade that flourished to circumvent official Spanish trade routes. Contraband became one of the sources of wealth for the Porteños (i.e., persons from Buenos Aires), and this in turn became the basis of the mercantile society that would, some 250 years later, push for political and economic independence.

ARGENTINA TODAY

What is today the Argentine Republic consists of the territories of the Viceroyalty of la Plata, which was created in 1776 to forestall the increasing sentiment of the Río de La Plata colonies that separation from Spain was desirable. What is today Paraguay (which declared its own independence in 1813) is what is left of the territories that were lost to Argentina and Brazil in a deadly war that occurred in the late 1870s. The republic of Uruguay was created in 1828 out of territory claimed by both Argentina and Brazil, with the idea that Uruguay would serve as a buffer state between the two largest countries of South America. Argentina continues to dispute certain land with Chile in the extreme southern tip of the hemisphere, and it continues to lay claims to the Falkland Islands (the Islas Malvinas), over which it fought a futile war with Great Britain in 1982.

Like the majority of Latin American societies, Argentina has experienced long-standing controversies over the importance of its major urban center. Ezequiel Martínez Estrada published an essay in 1940, *La cabeza de Goliat* (Goliath's Head), in which he used the biblical metaphor to characterize Argentina as a country suffering from hyperencephalitis (an unhealthy enlargement of the head). Indeed, today, one third of the country's population of thirty-four million resides in Greater Buenos Aires, and another third is concentrated along the river network that extends north and northwestward from the Buenos Aires delta, leaving barely ten million to populate the remaining vast stretches of the country. There is a famous saying to the effect that "God is everywhere, but he only holds office hours in Buenos Aires," a reference not only to how much of the population is concentrated in Buenos Aires, but also how the capital controls so much of the life of the nation.

BUENOS AIRES

Buenos Aires is not only the largest city of the country and the center for virtually every sphere of national life, it is a port city. Although one theme of Argentine culture is the isolation of Buenos Aires from the other major centers of the world—only recently has it been possible to reach Buenos Aires from the Northern Hemisphere in less than twenty-four hours by plane—Buenos Aires is also a major seaport. The role played by the city in the national consciousness is not only to represent the European (and, more recently, the U.S.) bases of Argentine society, arts, and culture but also to provide a convenient scapegoat on those occasions when Argentina is regarded as too European (or American), too international at the expense of a nationalistic consciousness, too urban and out of touch with its native roots, too committed to the sophistication (cynicism, worldliness, frivolity) of a large metropolis, and not sufficiently supportive of the values of the common folk. (Whether these positions are sociologically accurate [to many foreigners, for example, Buenos Aires's striving to be the Paris, New York, or Miami of the South could be dismissed as lamentably derivative, if not downright ridiculous] is less important than whether these are organizing principles of national positions that are often heatedly debated and, more than once, have been the basis of major political events.)

One is not speaking here of the hardly useful division between right and left, since, for example, a commitment to Creole national identity, to the authentically Argentine and Latin American, was a theme in both the guerrilla movement of the 1960s and 1970s and of the neofascist military dictatorship of the 1970s and 1980s. Equally, supporters of the former endorsed

An urbane Buenos Aires downtown-street scene. Courtesy of Eduardo Gil.

a return to humble origins at the same time that reactionaries and conservatives spoke of some sort of natural man who would intuitively reject the reasonings of the left-wing intellectuals. Furthermore, the interplay between internationalism and nationalism does not sort itself out along the lines of a fixed spectrum; both the right wing and the left wing have customarily denounced U.S. interference in internal affairs (although not always referring to the same phenomena). Buenos Aires routinely serves as a point of reference for these positions. The texture of life in both concrete and abstract terms necessarily involves an urban area in which all of the lines of power, material as well as symbolic, are densely intertwined. For example, something as simple as day-to-day shopping can be highly instructive for anyone who has followed the changes occurring in Argentine society for the past thirty years. One can examine which products are available (or not available), what kinds of establishments they are obtained from, and what the organization is (including advertising) of the establishments that provide them.

Part of the controversy over the nature of Buenos Aires has to do with the role of immigration in the formation of Argentine society. Although significant immigrant groups have settled outside Buenos Aires (Germans around the lake area on the central border with Chile; Irish, Scottish, and Welsh shepherds in Patagonia; Italian and Jewish farmers in the Mesopotamian area due north of Buenos Aires), most immigrants have, in fact, settled in Buenos Aires, first in distinctly ethnic enclaves and subsequently, with upward mobility, across social and class boundaries. The concern with immigration here is with the symbolic function immigration has had for various contexts of Argentine history.

IMMIGRANT GROUPS

Most immigrants in Argentina belong to one of three very distinctive groups, each one of which casts a different perspective on debates about the city. The original Creoles were, of course, almost exclusively of Spanish stock, with a smattering of other European nationalities. The African slaves who were brought in provided the first postconquest immigration. Although the presence of a black component of Argentine culture is part of the historical record, it has become a cultural cliché embedded in negative stereotypes. The controversy over what happened to the descendants of these slaves continues. The perennial proposition that those who did not perish in the wars of independence and the war fought by Argentina, Brazil, and Uruguay against Paraguay in the 1870s died from disease and overwork is probably inaccurate. The disease part of the proposition smacks of racial discrimination (inferior and therefore less healthy blacks), and their disappearance feeds a racist dream: when the blacks were no longer useful as slaves, they conveniently disappeared. More reasonable is the proposition that many blacks merged with other groups on the social fringes—the indigenous population (including mestizos—people of mixed blood) and poor Creole outcasts—to form an undifferentiated class of social outcasts. For this reason, *negro* in Argentine Spanish usually means a "nonwhite" rather than just a person of African descent; it may be applied to any nonprosperous immigrant, including Italians, Arabs, Jews, those from southern Spain, and so on.

The second principal immigrant group comprises Italians. Indeed, a major theme in Argentine history has been to claim that Argentina is the second homeland of Italians, and even the most superficial check of the Buenos Aires telephone directory would seem to confirm this fact. Once concentrated in certain sectors of the city (and, outside Buenos Aires, in the vast coastal region along the river network), people of Italian descent now constitute essentially the basic population of the capital and a large array of other major urban centers and surrounding areas (Rosario, for example, is often called the Chicago of Argentina). Italian may no longer be extensively spoken in Buenos Aires, but many claim to understand it, and various Italian dialects have made

The Casa Rosada (Pink House) is the seat of the Executive Branch of government. The third-floor balcony is famous for speeches by Juan Domingo Perón and his wife, Eva Duarte de Perón. Courtesy of Eduardo Gil.

significant lexical contributions to *Porteño*, "the local," Spanish. Tango lyrics are probably the greatest popular-culture repository of that immigrant culture and its linguistic impact on the nation. Finally, despite Argentina's legendary beef culture, Italian food basically dominates the Argentine diet—even more so with the decline in the last ten years of the availability to many Argentines of prime beef cuts.

Juan Domingo Perón, who was president of Argentina from 1946 until his overthrow by the military in 1955, was of Italian descent. Despite a history of its upper ranks being open only to the sons of the Creole elite, the Argentine armed forces, between 1966 and 1983, provided the majority of the ruling juntas' top-command officers of first- and second-generation Italian descent. It is important to underscore here how populism melded urban immigrant groups and rural provincials in a coalition with a broad labor and other lower-middle-class base into one of the most important political movements in Argentine history.[1]

The third most important immigrant group, which arrived after the early black slaves and the nineteenth-century Italian migrants are the Jews. Although Sephardic or Mediterranean Jews have been present in Latin America since the time of the Spanish Conquest, German and East European (commonly called Russian) Jews were also part of the large migration beginning around 1880 that included Italians. Part of a governmental policy functioned under the rubric "to govern is to populate," whereby not only a vast underpopulated geographic area would be inhabited, but indigenous peoples, mestizos, blacks, and marginal-class Creoles would be "civilized" thanks to the importation of new immigrant stocks. In time, the arrival of Jews in the Río de la Plata region resulted in Argentina becoming the largest center of Jewish culture in Latin America and one of the largest Jewish centers in the world (the most inclusive count ranks Buenos Aires as the fourth largest).

There continues, however, to be much anti-Semitism in Argentina (as elsewhere in Latin America). The Israeli embassy was bombed in 1992 and the Asociación Mutual Israelita Argentina (AMIA), a major cultural center, was bombed in 1994. There were many deaths in both cases and, so far, there have been no convictions. The Jewish presence nevertheless remains very strong, not only in all walks of life (in academic, intellectual, and artistic endeavors; in business; and in Argentina's well-developed entertainment industries), but also in the specifically Jewish institutions. The need for greater security after the bombings, especially the destruction of the AMIA center, led to the inventorying of hundreds of sites where Jews assemble in the city.

Until constitutional changes were made in the mid-1990s, the president was obliged to be a member of the Catholic Church. The Church has been a potent conservative and reactionary force in social and cultural politics. One example of this power is the ongoing historical debate it has provoked concerning mandatory Christian education in public schools. As a consequence, the historical tensions between Argentina as the major Jewish cultural setting in Latin America and Argentina's traditional Christian institutions are great.

Other immigrant strains in Argentina explain certain historical constants and provide important symbolic issues in sociocultural debates. The current president, Carlos Menem, comes from the large Arabic community that has strongholds in provinces lying west between Buenos Aires and the Andes. Many Spaniards came to Argentina as a result of the economic and political turmoil in Spain after World War I and during and after the civil war of the 1930s. Recent decades have seen an older Japanese population complemented by immigrants from Korea and Indochina. Indeed, with the upward mobility that has occurred in Argentina following the return in 1983 to constitutional democracy, Jews have been able to leave the traditional ghetto just west of downtown and move uptown and into the suburbs. Thousands of Korean immigrants have moved into the old Jewish quarter.

Historically, the Argentine sociocultural consciousness has had little to say about the country's indigenous population, either the groups that existed at the time of the Conquest or their present-day descendants. Various forms of cultural nationalism have included an interest in indigenous cultures and cultural production in some of the provinces; especially those along the border with Chile, Bolivia, Paraguay, and Brazil demonstrate a heightened sensitivity to the indigenous substratum. Yet there has never been in Argentina anything like an ideology of mestizo culture, such as the one Mexico has, with varying success, officially modeled subsequent to the 1910 revolution. Thus, from the perspective of Buenos Aires, one must make do with a handful of words (very small by comparison with Mexican and Andean Spanish or Brazilian Portuguese) drawn from indigenous languages, with some prominent folksingers, and with the *bombo*, the body-carried base drum Peronismo took from indigenous culture as one of its privileged icons.

David Viñas, one of Argentina's leading intellects who is famous for his incisive sociopolitical interpretations that involve the understanding of the social fabric through an interpretation of cultural production, claimed, when there was much discussion in Argentina and abroad about the "disappeared," that Argentina's indigenous peoples must be viewed as the first victims of the processes, both official and quasi-official, of disappearance. Viñas was attempting to underscore a correlation between the persecution, including detention, torture, and murder, of political dissidents in the 1970s and the 1879 Expedition to the Desert. The expedition resulted in the elimination of native Americans who were resisting attempts from Buenos Aires to settle the Pampas, which was necessary to establish Argentina's vast cattle industry. However, as Viñas would be the first to recognize, the disappearance of indigenous people is quite a bit more extensive than one horrendous military operation of extermination. The systematic silencing of or, at the very least, the undervaluing of Argentina's indigenous cultural heritage provides an important contextual reference for both its overall social imagination and, specifically, its cultural production. The theme that there is no racial conflict in Argentina is a potent one. It was widely cited during the period of civil unrest in the United States by those Argentines who defended the military dictatorship and questioned the consequences of democracy. American-style democracy led American to civil unrest, whereas the sober authoritarianism of Argentina held society in focus around an official version of a stable national identity in which racial and ethnic differences disappeared. Critics of both the military in general and this Argentine version of racial politics were, like Viñas (himself of Jewish roots), quick to point out periods of intense racial and ethnic conflict in Argentina. These included the Tragic Week in 1919, when a rampage led by ultranationalist groups against Jews and Jewish establishments foreshadowed Germany's 1938 *Kristallnacht*, when Nazi troops went on a rampage destroying Jewish property and synagogues. The fact that so many of those who constituted Perón's populist base were either first-generation immigrants or were indigenous and mestizo provincials brought to Buenos Aires by Peronista social policies meant that this class conflict bore a deep racial and ethnic imprint.

One of the linguistic legacies of Peronismo is the phrase *cabecita negras* (blackhead). The term was created by the opponents of Perón as a slur against provincials, mostly from the north of the country, who were encouraged, often with free train tickets, to pour into Buenos Aires. Economically, the idea was that they would become a pliant new workforce in the industrialization projects envisioned by Perón, as well as employees in the expanding statist infrastructure. In sociopolitical terms, the goal was to challenge the European ("white") supremacy of Buenos Aires and to impose, no matter how clumsily, a sense of continuity between the self-styled, sophisticated port city and the vast outback of the country. The children and grandchildren of this internal migration, fifty years later, now constitute a significant demographic identity within the nation's capital and surrounding suburbs.

Justification of the internal migration of indigenous people and mestizos, often through popular-culture formats like television and film, has had important consequences for a sociopolitically committed cultural production in Argentina. A term like *cabecita negra*, originally coined as a racial insult, can be resemanticized, seized by the very group it was meant to oppress, and used as a term of cultural capital. One does not need to invest in the proposition that the *cabecitas negras* are the "real" Argentines to understand that the exclusion of them from the social, political, and, particularly, cultural records is an act of disappearance. Such forms of disappearance may not be as brutal or final as the disappearance of political dissidents in the 1970s, which created the transitive verb *desaparecer*, "to disappear someone or to make someone disappear." Yet for the daily life of an individual, the deprivation of symbolic meaning, the sense of having no meaningful existence within the symbolic structure of a society, is indeed a form of brutality with enormous social and psychological consequences. It is for this reason that ethnic and racial identity, about which there is silence in Argentine society, and class conflict, with its enormous dimensions of ethnicity, constitute major issues of the Argentine historical context, as can be ascertained from both the silences and the eloquences of that country's cultural production.

The question of the disappeared arose in the context of one of the many periods of tyrannical government in Argentina since, at the very least, the first nationalist and fascist-inspired military coup in 1930. For many historians and cultural commentators, the fact that Argentina did not have military governments during the 100 years of its history prior to the 1930 coup is not in itself comforting, since the twin issues of systematic disenfranchisement (class and gender based and regional) and electoral fraud (the ward-boss, *compadrito* [buddy], deliver-the-vote system) hardly meant that prior to 1930 Argentina was a model representative democracy. Indeed, the military movement that brought Perón to power, first in secondary positions and then as president in 1946, insisted as one of its bases for legitimation that it was combating the political corruption of the many governments, civilian and military, that followed in the wake of the 1930 coup. Moreover, subsequent military coups have routinely claimed legitimacy by alleging that their institutional integrity was greater than that of the civilian political process.

MILITARISM AND AUTHORITARIANISM

The related themes of militarism and authoritarianism have provided topics for Argentine social and cultural history. Militarism refers not only to the influence of the armed forces in national life—an influence that derives as much from the role of the military in the creation of Argentina as it does from the ways in which the armed forces have generated for themselves material and symbolic power in the context of national affairs over almost 200 years of national history. It refers also to the ways in which various parallel institutions—the Church, the schoolhouse, the work place, the labor union—may not always reveal the same sort of hierarchical authority and demands for allegiance and obedience as do the institutional armed forces. It refers to how those parallel institutions may be militarized—their relative degree of susceptibility to militarization or resistance to it—during periods of the armed takeover of government.

Authoritarianism, while it is an integral part of militarism, is more free-floating, and is taken to mean the relative degree of trust in and support of a principal authority, whether in the concrete sphere of the wielding of power or in the symbolic sphere of discursive privilege. *"Aquí somos todos hijos del rigor"* (Here we're all children who know how to toe the line) is one motif of Argentine culture. Certainly, it is questioned during periods of resistance to authority, military or otherwise. Equally, it is a byword that refers to the need to accept authority in a well-ordered society, a proposition to which the hierarchical left as much as the hierarchical right can subscribe. By the same token, Argentina has a long anarchist tradition that one can relate, historically, to Jewish, Italian, and Spanish immigrant influence. Indeed, the persecution of anarchists in the early twentieth century had as much to do with anti-immigrant and anti-Semitic sentiment as it did with anarchism as a political threat. One could almost say that, from the point of view of symbolic capital, anarchism in Argentina today is an ideology that has become invested with considerable romantic nostalgia. By contrast, most of the traditional left, in any of its versions, has virtually no such cachet. It is questionable whether even Argentina's Che Guevara, the most admired figure of the revolutionary guerilla movement of the 1960s, has much iconic value left at all. Of course, there continues to be a well entrenched intellectual left in Argentina, associated primarily with the universities and various institutes and think-tanks. Driven by complex theories of cultural process and production, this left, with its extensive international connections, is a far cry from the Revolutionary People's Army and other similar groups of a quarter of a century ago.

Virtually all societies reveal an extensive awareness of their political institutions and their workings, as seen in scientific and cultural production, and in both high and low culture. Argentina is no exception. There is probably no other society in Latin America (nor in most of Europe) made up of such avid readers of newspapers and magazines, which results in a fairly complex national dialogue over politics. However, authoritarianism and the special social circumstances it creates, including militarism and the periodic exercise by the armed forces of absolute authority, provides for one of the macrocontexts of Argentine history, as can also be seen by the extensive bibliography relating to it.

PRESIDENT DOMINGO FAUSTINO SARMIENTO

By Latin American standards, Argentina enjoys a very high level of education. Schoolteacher President Domingo Faustino Sarmiento (who held office from 1862–1869) left the country with the triple legacy of an education that was to be lay, free, and mandatory, at least through primary school. A high percentage of Argentines complete secondary school, particularly in urban areas. University education (as well as vocational tertiary education) is, basically speaking, readily available. Although many aspects of Argentine life previously supported by the state have been privatized as part of the neoliberalist policies of Carlos Menem (president since 1989), education continues to be a state enterprise, which means that it is mostly free or very inexpensive. It also means that the Argentine educational system suffers from all of the infrastructure problems of statism and budgetary neglect. Yet, there is a traditional reverence for education in Argentina and respect both for public and Church-related institutions, as well as for the myriad private schools and universities that have emerged in recent decades (especially business and technological schools supported by the neoliberalist process). Intellectual life, particularly in Buenos Aires, is strong and vibrant. Books may no longer be as readily available a commodity as they once were, but a quick comparison with the book trade in other Latin American capitals reveals how extensive publishing and book selling continue to be in Argentina.

One of Sarmiento's other legacies will serve to close this brief overview of the social, political, and cultural contexts of Argentina. During the period in which Sarmiento was in exile in Chile in the 1840s (where he was first involved in public education and the preparation of normal school teachers), he published numerous broadsides against the dictator Juan Manuel de Rosas (who exercised power essentially between 1829 and 1852). One of these became a founding text of Argentine literature and Sarmiento's most famous text, the sociological treatise cum narrative: *Civilización i barbarie* (Civilization and Barbarism, 1848; published in English as *Life in the Argentine Republic in the Days of the Tyrants*), better known as *Facundo*. Facundo Quiroga was a provincial warlord whose legendary status Sarmiento interpreted to signify an abiding allegiance to Argentina, several decades after the republic was established under, in part, the sign of Francmasonry. Sarmiento saw this barbarism as appalling and as a deadly holdover from the Spanish presence in Latin America. Sarmiento urged his readers to agree with him and to endorse the need to enhance an enlightened European, non-Mediterranean tradition for Argentina, which would, of course, come from universal education and the advancement of the social sciences. Close readings of *Facundo* reveal that Sarmiento himself was not immune to the charisma of Facundo and the cultural values he represented, but his book has come to be viewed as crucial to debates in Argentina over national culture versus foreign imports, the traditional values of the countryside/outback and the urban sophistication of the metropolis, and the Hispanic versus the non-Hispanic; in short, of barbarism versus civilization. Real social and cultural history, to be sure, has little use for such neat dichotomies, but the practices of symbolic capital often do, frequently in dramatic ways.

Sarmiento's Argentine barbarism is characterized by the gaucho, the legendary nomadic plainsmen who were the abandoned offspring of indigenous women and Spanish soldiers. The nomadism of the gauchos and the primitive conditions of their lifestyle made them a suitable symbol first for the degenerate human stock created by the Spanish conquest and second of a social infrastructure that could be improved only by the importation of non-

Hispanic European ideas and immigrants. Gauchos had served, however, as military irregulars in the war of independence, and they subsequently constituted the power base of the regional caudillos like Facundo. José Hernández's poem *Martín Fierro* (1872, 1879), with its virtually epic proportions, contributed to the creation of a romantic myth of the gaucho as a figure of the authentic Argentine, a process continued by the novel *Don Segundo Sombra* (1926) by Ricardo Güiraldes and a host of subsequent official and popular cultural versions of the gaucho. It is significant that both Hernández and Güiraldes were wealthy landowners, a fact that confirms how the gaucho progressed from being the pariah of Sarmiento's characterization to becoming, along with the tango, one of the great Argentine cultural icons of the twentieth century.

Sarmiento's disjunction of civilization versus barbarism, with his unrelenting and unmistakable claim of the superiority of the former, allows one to see the extent to which foreign culture holds a secure yet complex place in the Argentine imagination. The mystique of French culture for generations of intellectuals, the sovereign dignity of the British imperial style for traditional oligarchy, and the seductive cornucopia of the American way of life for much of the middle class are all important ingredients in Argentine self-identity, not merely foreign influences. Also, the French and English languages have exercised an enormous symbolic, as well as practical, allure. Teaching these languages has led to the establishment of important cultural institutions and a flourishing cottage industry of language instruction. Under the backing of neoliberalist economic policies, the sway of American English is at the moment unquestionable.

THE THEME OF EXILE

The other side of the coin of the interaction between Argentina and foreign cultures is the recurring theme of exile. There have been many periods through Argentine history in which combinations of political, economic, and social factors have led to exile as either a relatively free choice or as the alternative to incarceration and perhaps death. Many Argentines, including Sarmiento, lived and worked outside Argentina during the Rosas dictatorship. For cultural reasons, many Argentines chose Europe over what they considered to be the limited resources of the homeland. The naturalist and local-color writer William Henry Hudson (known to the Argentines as Guillermo Enrique Hudson) preferred to reside in England and to write in English. The Peronist period produced its own exile population; the Paris-based Julio Cortázar was the most prominent of these (Cortázar, however, never abandoned the Spanish language). The military period of the 1970s and 1980s produced a large emigration, and well-trained Argentine professionals have long found relatively easy employment in the United States and Europe.

A related issue of exile is the way in which Argentina has served as a place of exile, both political and economic, for other Latin Americans. For example, after the 1973 military coup in Chile, many Chileans sought refuge in Buenos Aires only to be forced to look elsewhere after the 1976 coup in Argentina. Although Paraguay now has a constitutional democracy, for more than forty years the country was under one of the worst dictatorships of the continent. As a consequence, more Paraguayans lived in Buenos Aires than in Asunción, the capital of Paraguay. (Brazil is another country with a large number of exiled Paraguayans.) But even discounting the phenomenon of exile, Argentina, with its relative prosperity, and Buenos Aires, with its relative cultural and social sophistication, have played, in the imagination of surrounding Latin American societies, the same symbolic role that France, Britain, and the United States have played for Argentina. And, just as there are Argentines who denounce dependency on foreign models, Argentina is as often scolded as it is idealized by its neighbors.

NOTE

1. Also to be discussed is Perón's wife, Eva Duarte de Perón, or Evita, who, until her untimely death at the age of thirty-three in 1952, worked to support the policies of her husband. A national and international cult has emerged around the figure of Evita—one that is as stridently denunciatory ("that whore") as it is idealizing ("Santa Evita"). Evita, as an illegitimate child and as a provincial, had to struggle to survive in Buenos Aires. Her life as a young woman was marked by irregularities unacceptable to bourgeois decency, including being Perón's public lover before their marriage. As the wife of the president who demanded her own public and political persona and an independent power base, and as an individual who seemed to go out of her way to defy conventions circumscribing woman's place in society, she has come, however, to provide Argentina with perhaps its most potent sociopolitical symbol.

REFERENCES

Argentina, la otra patria de los italianos/Argentina, l'altra patria deglia italiani. Proyecto y dirección/Progetto e direzione Manrique Zago. Buenos Aires: Manrique Zago Ediciones, 1983.

Ball, Deirdre, ed. *Argentina.* Directed and designed by Hans Hoefer. Singapore: APA Publications, 1988.

Estrada, Ezequiel Martínez. *La Cabeza de Goliat.* Buenos Aires: Club del Libro, 1990.

Foster, David William. *Buenos Aires: City and Culture.* Gainesville: University Press of Florida, 1998 (forthcoming).

Martínez, Tomás Eloy. *The Perón Novel.* Trans. by Asa Zatz. New York: Pantheon Books, 1988.

———. *Santa Evita.* Trans. by Helen Lane. New York: Alfred A. Knopf, 1996.

Page, Joseph A. *Perón: A Biography.* New York: Random House, 1983.

The Redemocratization of Argentine Culture, 1983 and Beyond; An International Research Symposium at Arizona State University, February 16–17, 1987. Proceedings edited by David William Foster. Tempe: Center for Latin American Studies, Arizona State University, 1989.

Rock, David. *Argentina 1516–1982, from Spanish Colonization to the Falklands War.* Berkeley: University of California Press, 1985.

———. *Authoritarian Argentina; The Nationalist Movement, Its History and Its Impact.* Berkeley: University of California Press, 1992.

Sarmiento, Domingo Faustino. *Civilización i barbarie.* Santiago: Imprenta del Progreso, 1845.

———. *Life in the Argentine Republic in the Days of the Tyrants.* New York: Hurd and Houghton, 1868.

Taylor, Julie M. *Eva Perón: The Myths of a Woman.* Chicago: University of Chicago Press, 1979.

Tenenbaum, Barbara A., ed. "Argentina." In *Encyclopedia of Latin American History and Culture.* 1:142–60. New York: Scribner's, 1996.

Viñas, David. *Indios, ejército y frontera.* Mexico City: Siglo Veintiuno Editores, 1982.

Weisbrot, Robert. *The Jews of Argentina: From the Inquisition to Perón.* Philadelphia: Jewish Publication Society of America, 1979.

Wheaton, Kathleen, ed. *Buenos Aires.* Directed and designed by Hans Hoefer. Singapore: APA Publications, 1988.

2

Religion

IN ARGENTINA, as in other Latin American countries, the overwhelming majority of its citizens (more than 90 percent) profess to be Roman Catholic. Argentina is rather unique, however, because the majority of its citizens are also substantially more secular than religious. This is most evident in Buenos Aires where the longtime joke is that the religion of Argentines is Freudianism. Although the popular saying is mainly intended to poke fun at the *Porteños'* proclivity for psychoanalysis, it would not be a stretch to argue more seriously that in many ways psychoanalytic theory has taken the place of religion in the lives of a large sector of the population.

Argentina does not have a form of popular Catholicism akin to that of Mexico, which developed around the Virgin of Guadalupe and evolved into a nationwide phenomenon that in and of itself is part of the national identity and integral to what it means to be Mexican. Nevertheless, Argentina is not without its own homegrown version of the miraculous appearance of the Virgin Mary who is said to have manifested herself in 1630 to a traveler. The story is that a man was transporting two statues of the Virgin from Brazil to Perú. While he was crossing a river near the city of Luján, his cart became bogged down in the mud. The cart finally was freed when one of the statues was removed to lighten the load. The man interpreted this experience as a sign that the Virgin wanted to remain there. A shrine was erected around the statue which became known as the Virgin of Luján. The original statue is now mounted above the altar of the immense basilica in Luján which was completed in 1935. Twice a year thousands of faithful believers carry out a pilgrimage covering the forty or so miles between Buenos Aires and Luján on foot. The images of the Virgin that can be seen adorning taxi cabs and *colectivos* (city buses) in Buenos Aires are of the Virgen de Luján.

CATHOLICISM

The Roman Catholic Church has been a dominant force in the social and political formation of Argentina, and traditionally it has played an important role in the government and the establishment of laws and public policy. This is particularly true following the rise of Catholic Nationalism, which began to take shape at the end of the nineteenth century. The Nationalist view of Argentina was one in which the union of church and state—the twin pillars of society—was seen as the only viable way to preserve the Hispano-Catholic cultural patrimony. The direction of Argentine politics over successive generations has been related directly to the Church, whether in support of it or in opposition to it. The roots of Catholic Nationalism can be traced back to the Generation of 1880, a group of intellectuals and government leaders who adhered closely to the ideals of positivism. They sought the complete separation of church and state, following the North American model, and they were successful in reducing to a minimum the role of the Catholic Church in secular society. The prevailing beliefs among this generation were centered on science (biological evolution), anticlericalism, and liberal democratic ideals.

The initial reaction of Catholics to liberalism came in the form of lay organizations that attempted to exert a moral Catholic influence on society through publications and charitable acts. Catholic elites, however, sought a more direct and immediate solution by forming a political party. As the traditional Catholics built up a powerful coalition they began to clash with the secular liberals, and the struggle to define the future of Argentina commenced. The large influx of immigrants brought trouble for the liberals, even though they saw it as a way to improve and civilize the country. However, with immigration came a number of problems that Catholics began to blame on the lack of traditional values which was further fed by an increasing fear of socialism, advocated by many of the immigrants. Catholic Nationalism became an actual movement in the 1920s. A number of other nationalist organizations began to spring up during this period as well.

One of the pivotal events of the period has come to be known as *La Semana Trágica* or the Tragic Week of 1919. It began with a strike by 2,500 employees of Pedro Vasena's iron mill. The workers began to strike during the first week of December 1918, demanding a reduction of the workday from eleven to eight hours, higher salaries, and Sundays off work. The strike continued until January 7, 1919, when a strike-breaking force, accompanied by the police, showed up at the factory to quell the rebellion. The ensuing fracas resulted in the deaths of several workers and the injury of many more. This provoked a massive general strike throughout the country, which escalated into a show of force between the police, the army, the government, and the upper class against the workers. It was widely held that the Russian workers (80 percent of whom were Jewish) were responsible for the social unrest. A civil group representing the elite and calling themselves the Guardia Blanca (White Guard) took it upon themselves to defend national priorities against the Russian socialists and anarchists. Other groups calling themselves the "defenders of order" joined in, and, most important, the Liga Patriótica Argentina (Argentine Patriotic League), one of the country's most nationalistic organizations, was formed. These groups launched virulent attacks on the Jewish neighborhoods of Buenos Aires, burning businesses and homes, as well as beating people at random, while the police passively looked the other way. The attack constituted the first true pogrom against the Jews in the Americas.

One of the most pernicious aspects of Catholic Nationalism was its extreme anti-Semitism, which David Rock has meticulously documented and which is summed up in the following statement: "For the Nationalists, Jews were 'the deadly enemies of the nation and of the Catholic faith of the people.' Jewish 'materialism' stood in irreconcilable opposition to the 'spiritual character' of the Latin peoples" (Rock 1992, 23). The coup led by General José Félix Uriburu, which ushered in the *década infame* (infamous decade), also heightened incidents of anti-Semitism. One of the most widely circulated pieces of literature was the bogus *The Protocols of the Elders of Zion* (also known as *The Protocols of the Wise Men of Zion*), published in 1905 at Tsarskoye Selo in a book by S. Nilus. Likewise, Gustavo Adolfo Martínez Zuviría (1883–1954), a fervent anti-Semite and director of the national library, wrote several vicious anti-Jewish books under the pseudonym of Hugo Wast; most famous among them is the two-part *Kahal* and *Oro* (1935). Martínez Zuviría was later appointed minister of justice and public instruction. In response to his literature, the Jewish poet and dramatist, César Tiempo (pseudonym of Israel Zeitlin [1906–1980]) wrote a scathing rejoinder titled *La campaña antisemita y el director de la Biblioteca Nacional* (The Anti-Semitic Campaign and the Director of the National Library; 1935). Successful coup d'états were carried out by Catholic Nationalist military officers—by General Eduardo Lonardi in 1955 and by General Juan Carlos Onganía in 1966.

Juan Perón had a turbulent relationship with the Catholic Church. During his first term, he actively promoted Catholicism and the goals of the Catholic Church through a number of programs that put the Church at the core of Argentine society, which of course appeased the Nationalists who more fervently than ever were waging a war to bring Catholicism back to its rightful place. However, during his second presidential term, Perón turned his back on the Catholic Church and took away many of the benefits and privileges he had previously restored. The Catholic Nationalists were infuriated and responded in force. The Vatican excommunicated Perón and several of his aides, and in 1955 he was overthrown by Lonardi.

JUDAISM

The military dictatorship known as the *Proceso de Reorganización Nacional* (Process of National Reorganization [1976–1983]) was one of the darkest periods of Argentine history, and in many ways it was the culmination of years of political conflict. While many priests and laymen within the Catholic Church were outwardly opposed to the dictatorship and even suffered at the hands of the military, it was generally believed and now known that many high-ranking Catholic officials worked in collusion with the military. As in previous periods of military rule, the *Proceso* was profoundly influenced by Nazi ideology. Probably nowhere is this explained in greater detail or with such passion than in Jacobo Timerman's testimonial narrative *Prisoner without a Name, Cell without a Number* (1981). Timerman was the editor of the newspaper *La Opinión* when he was kidnapped by a paramilitary death squad. After being held prisoner for several months, he was freed thanks to international pressure, but he was stripped of his citizenship and put on a plane to Israel. In his account of the experience, Timerman elaborates on the wild Jewish conspiracy theories believed wholeheartedly by the military generals. One of the goals of the military was to rid Argentina of the subversive ideologies of the evil Jewish triumvirate—Sigmund Freud, Albert Einstein, and Karl Marx—who had tried to destroy the Christian concept of the family, the concept of time and space, and the concept of society, respectively (Timerman 1981, 139).

As Timerman posited, the military mentality was informed by anti-Jewish myths and conspiracy theories, many based on the *Protocols of the Elders of Zion*. Military leaders were convinced that Argentine Zionism was part of a much larger conspiracy with Israel, known as the Plan Andinia, to take control of Patagonia, the southern region of the country, in order to establish a second Jewish state (Kaufman and Cymberknopf 1989, 255–56). This was to be the start of World War III, according to the generals. It was common, therefore, to interrogate Jewish prisoners about their knowledge of the Plan Andinia (Kaufman and Cymberknopf 1989; Comisión Nacional Sobre la Desaparación de Personas 1992; Timerman 1981).

It would be erroneous to maintain that Jews were routinely abducted by paramilitary squads solely because they were Jews. Nevertheless, it has been documented that Jewish prisoners received "special treatment" because they were Jews (Siminovich 1989). Jewish prisoners were subjected to a barrage of humiliations and tortures infused with Nazi symbolism that non-Jewish prisoners were not made to suffer: swastikas were worn by military men or painted on the prisoner's body; prisoners were made to kneel before images of Adolf Hitler; constant references were made to Hitler, the SS, and the Gestapo; and prisoners were repeatedly threatened with being made into soap (Kaufman and Cymberknopf 1989, 249–56; Comisión 1992, 69–75).

While Jews may not have been arrested for being Jewish, they constituted a disproportionate number of prisoners in relation to the general population. Jews make up approximately 1 percent of the total population of Argentina; however, as many as 10 percent of the estimated 30,000 people tortured or killed during the dictatorship were Jewish (Kaufman and Cymberknopf 1989, 256–60).

Following the return to institutional democracy, the newly elected president, Raúl Alfonsín, had to be very careful in regard to the steps he would take to ensure justice and maintain good relations with the Catholic Church. Those initial troubling times are now a thing of the past, and the course of Catholicism seems to have stabilized and become much less reactionary. One of the most controversial issues related to the Church was the legalization of divorce. In protest some 50,000 Catholics, led by Bishop Ogñenovich, demonstrated by carrying the Virgin of Luján from the basilica to the metropolitan cathedral in the Plaza de Mayo in central Buenos Aires. This was only the second time in 400 years that the statue of the Virgin had been removed (Burdick 1995, 243). The most complete study of the Catholic Church in twentieth-century Argentina is found in *For God and the Fatherland: Religion and Politics in Argentina* (1995) by Michael A. Burdick. The author traces the development of Catholicism from the nineteenth century to the present by way of the Nationalist movements, Perón, and the *Proceso*.

Jews constituted a significant immigrant group in Argentina. The end of the nineteenth century for the Jews of Eastern Europe, Russia, and the Mediterranean was a period of upheaval marked by aggressive pogroms which caused them to initiate a massive migration westward. Many of these migrating Jews fleeing persecution arrived in the Río de la Plata region. Between the late 1880s and World War I, an enormous colonization effort was taking place in Argentina, and to a lesser extent in Uruguay, Brazil, and the United States. This venture was the brainchild of the extremely wealthy Jewish philanthropist Baron Maurice de Hirsch. Hirsch organized and funded the Jewish Colonization Association (JCA) in 1889, which encouraged and assisted Jews fleeing the Old World strife to settle on agricultural colonies established mainly in the littoral region of Argentina in the provinces of Entre Ríos, Santa Fe, and Buenos Aires. The earliest attempts at Jewish agricultural settlements were dismal failures; however, Hirsch believed he could solve the problems. The first and most famous agricultural settlement, Moisesville, was not actually founded by the baron, but the example set by its founders convinced him that it was a viable endeavor. By the time the baron died in 1896 the JCA had acquired some 750,000 acres of land in Argentina on which 6,757 colonists had settled. The first group of colonists to arrive under the auspices of Baron Hirsch consisted of 824 passengers aboard the ocean liner *Weser* which made port in Buenos Aires on August 24, 1889. They were the first group of Jews to arrive en masse in Argentina and were some of the founding pioneers of many of the first Jewish agricultural colonies in the country. While most were elated to have escaped the hardships of their homeland, many were disappointed to discover that life in the agricultural colonies was not the rural utopia they had envisioned. Life was extremely difficult on their farms. Hardships, including bad harvests, insect plagues of biblical proportions that devoured crops, and occasional hostility from the Creole population, were endured. Perhaps the most difficult stumbling block came from the JCA itself, which, following the death of the baron, seemed overrun by corruption and unfair treatment of the colonists, many of whom experienced serious financial failure.

As the years passed, many colonists discovered that life in Buenos Aires was better than eking out a living on the farm, and slowly the colonies began to diminish in size or disappear altogether. The failure of the agricultural settlements is explained by a variety of reasons. Many contend that the Jewish settlers simply did not have practical experience as farmers. Most had come from cities originally and were accustomed to making a living in urban settings as businessmen, salesmen, or craftsmen. One may wonder why the Jews were so eager to take up an agricultural life if they had no prior experience in farming. The explanation is to be found in the currents of Jewish thought at the turn of the century. Three major ideas were developed: Zionism, the creation of a Jewish homeland; an emphasis on the spiritual unity of Jews throughout the diaspora; and a return to nature and to productive labor on the land. Jews, therefore, were eager to renew their spiritual connection with the land as well as to find a place of their own.

The philanthropy of the JCA was really a feudalist system that made the colonists dependent tenants rather than independent farmers. As the price of the land rose, however, many colonists found their way out by selling the land, making a profit, and migrating to the city. The most important reason for migrating to the city was the lack of schooling in the remote Pampas. For the Jewish colonists, education was a concrete cultural imperative that far outweighed any abstract devotion to the land. No matter the failures, the Jewish colonists persevered in the early stages, and the agricultural colonies served the purpose of orienting the new immigrants gradually to their new environment rather than forcing them immediately to learn a new language, new social attitudes, and different cultural codes that life in the city would have demanded.

The children of the immigrants were able to emerge into mainstream Argentine culture secure in their abilities to "make it in America." Assimilation, however, proved to be a constant source of conflict between first- and second-generation Argentine Jews. The children were eager to leave Old World Jewry behind and join the modern world, while parents struggled to cling to the remaining vestiges of Jewish tradition which they saw as rapidly vanishing. Intermarriage became a serious threat to the survival of the Jewish community, and even today it is seen by the more conservative sectors of the Argentine Jewish population as a threat to Jewish continuity. The history of the Jewish agricultural colonies today is often seen in almost mythical terms, yet however glossed over the realities of the experiment, there can be no denying the importance of these early Jewish settlements.

The early immigrants paved the way for subsequent generations to become firmly established in Argentina. The participation of Jews within all areas of Argentine cultural and scientific activity has been vast. In spite of barriers, Jews have been become prominent figures in Argentine culture, particularly in the arts. An immense body of Jewish writers, actors, musicians, filmmakers, and television and radio personalities have made considerable contributions to the cultural makeup of modern-day Argentina. Jews have also been very prominent in the fields of science, medicine, sports, and journalism.

The Argentine Jewish community is not only the largest in Latin America, but the fifth largest in the world. The estimation of the exact size of the Jewish population of Argentina has varied between 200,000 and 500,000; the most realistic appraisal seems to be in the neighborhood of from 250,000 to 300,000. There are sixty-one synagogues and five major institutions along with numerous schools. On July 18, 1994, a terrorist bomb completely destroyed the seven-story building that housed the Asociación Mutual Israelita Argentina (AMIA, the Jewish Mutual Aid Society), killing nearly 100 people.

Immediately following the incident, news reports began to tally up the number of Jews killed and the number of "innocent victims." Similarly, certain groups and individuals began to call for all Jewish institutions, schools, and businesses to be moved to one sector of the city where they would not pose a threat to the rest of the neighborhood; essentially the idea was to ghettoize the Jewish population (Horovitz 1994). The tragedy was a somber reminder that anti-Semitism is very much still a part of Argentine reality. Two years prior to the AMIA bombing, a car bomb destroyed the Israeli embassy in Buenos Aires. There was widespread support in Argentina following the AMIA bombing, a large demonstration in the Plaza del Congreso, and demonstrations each year on the anniversary, but as of now there have been no convictions and the whole investigation has been embroiled in scandal. In fact, the federal police have been linked to the bombing (Salinas 1997).

The majority of the Argentine Jewish community is highly secular. Many of the Jews who immigrated to Argentina were not very religious, and in the process of assimilation most have lost any meaningful connection with Judaism; nevertheless, most maintain a very ethnic cultural identity as Jews. As alternatives to Judaism, many Jews in Argentina have embraced Marxism or Zionism as a kind of religion.

High-profile Jewish intellectuals have often been cast in the role of community leaders or spokespersons. Chief among them is Jacobo Timerman, but to an even greater extent Marcos Aguinis (b. 1935) has come to be considered an intellectual leader in the Jewish community and in Argentina in general. Aguinis played a key role in the process of redemocratization first as the subsecretary to culture and then as the secretary. He was responsible for putting into action the Programa Nacional de Democratización de la Cultura (PRONDEC, or National Program for the Democratization of Culture), a program designed to help ease the country back into democracy. Aguinis was eventually dismissed from his position as secretary of culture amid much controversy, some of which stemmed from the fact that he is Jewish. Aguinis is a prolific essayist and novelist. His most recent novel, *La matriz del infierno* (The womb of hell, 1997), chronicles the rise of Nazism in Argentina during the first half of the century. His essays are widely read in Argentina and typically are reprinted several times. His two most famous essays are *Carta esperanzada a un general* (Hopeful letter to a general, 1983), an eloquently written essay in which he utilizes the trope of epistolary writing in order to examine the mentality of the military leaders; and *Un país de novela: viaje hacia la mentalidad de los argentinos* (A fictional country: Voyage into the Argentine mentality, 1988). In *Un país de novela*, Aguinis traces the major trends and events of Argentine history and calls for the need to establish a pluralistic society in Argentina if the country is to advance. As evidence of Aguinis's role as a religious leader of sorts is his book-length dialogue with Monsignor Justo Laguna in which they discuss topics that include Jewish-Christian relations, Argentine history, the armed forces, religion and ideology, postmodernity, and politicians. The volume, *Diálogos sobre la Argentina y el fin del milenio* (Dialogues about Argentina and the end of the millennium, 1996) had been widely read and discussed in Argentina.

Santiago Kovadloff (b. 1942) is another Jewish intellectual whose writing has made a significant impact on Argentine culture, most specifically during and after the *Proceso*. One of his most well-known essays is *"Un lugar en el tiempo: la Argentina como vivencia de los judíos"* (A place in time: Argentina as the lived experience of the Jews), which appears in *La nueva ignorancia*. It is not only one of his best essays on a Jewish topic, but it is perhaps the most cogent essay written by anyone in Argentina on the problematics of Jewish-Argentine identity. Like Aguinis, Kovadloff repeatedly emphasizes the need for greater cultural pluralism. Along the same line is the recent collection of essays by Ricardo Feierstein (b. 1942): *Contraexilio y mestizaje: ser judío en la Argentina* (Counterexile and Mestizaje: To be Jewish in Argentina, 1996). Feierstein is most concerned with (re)defining Jewish identity in Argentina. Working with the racial hybridity concept of *mestizaje* (the mixture of races), he has come up with a theory for what one may call the "Arjewtine."

Since Jewish identity is defined more along the lines of culture and ethnicity than in terms of religiosity in Argentina, literature has proven to be an important vehicle for transmitting cultural values, recording histories, and preserving traditions. Argentina has one of the richest concentrations of Jewish literature in the world, with more than 300 established writers. Jewish authors in Argentina are fundamental to the evolutionary process of identity formation. As they grapple with the past and explicate the present they are helping to shape the future with a sense of purpose that takes on religious dimensions.

CULT OF EVA PERÓN

One can easily speak of the larger-than-life figure of Eva Perón within the context of popular religion. Argentines often refer to the "myth of Eva Perón" or even the "cult of Eva Perón," and many of her faithful supporters revere her with the title Santa Evita. Julie M. Taylor points to the religious connotations associated with Evita at the very onset of her book *Eva Perón: The Myths of a Woman.*

Both in Argentina and abroad, it was widely believed that the myth of Evita had arisen in the Argentinian working classes and centered an ideal of pure and passive womanhood incarnate, who exercised saintly power closely related to this classic femininity. According to this idea, popular enthusiasm for Eva Perón not only assumes a vaguely religious nature, but also takes the form of an irrational, mystic reverence for a saint or madonna. (Taylor 1979, 1)

Commemorations marking the date of her death often resemble religious revivals with the faithful singing the "Marcha Peronista," sermonlike speeches honoring her memory, a good amount of wailing and crying, and always the moment of silence at 8:25 P.M., the exact time of her death. Her presence is conjured up with the chant "se siente, se siente, Evita está presente" (you can feel it, you can feel it, Evita is among us). Her final resting place in La Recoleta Cemetery, though not the most elaborate tomb there, is considered a shrine to those who follow the cult of Evita. Her untimely death at the age of thirty-three preserved the saintly image she and others had so carefully crafted during her lifetime.

The working classes, her devout *descamisados*, were hungry to accept her extraordinary acts of generosity. They had always been on the margins of society, and when Juan and Eva Perón placed them at the very center, they won their unwavering devotion and harnessed their tremendous political power. Rumors began to circulate that Evita was capable of almost superhuman accomplishments and that she wielded a sort of divine power; the rumors were soon elevated to the status of myth. The cult of Eva Perón was and is replete with accompanying songs, images, quotations, and other symbols that have perpetuated the myth surrounding her. What has survived to the present day is more the myth of Eva Perón than the reality. Most Argentines, and even more so foreigners, find it difficult to separate fact from fiction when it comes to the former first lady of Argentina. The recent resurgence of interest in Evita (brought about by the Hollywood film and the Argentine response to it, *Eva Perón* [1996]) has produced a fair number of objective histories. One of the best, *Eva Perón: la biografía*, was written by Alicia Dujovne Ortiz in 1995. Ultimately, the many factions of Peronism as well as other political parties have constructed the version of Eva Perón that best suits their ideological needs. Eva Perón as a religious-political icon is what dominates the Argentine imagination.

PROTESTANTISM

It is generally believed that Protestant religions in Argentina are a relatively new phenomenon because recent decades have witnessed a great surge in

Protestantism throughout Argentina, although the growth here is occurring at a slower rate than in other Latin American countries. In fact, however, the Protestant presence in the country dates back to the nineteenth century with the arrival of various different immigrant groups. These groups brought with them the religions of their countries of origin and established in Argentina a variety of ethnic Protestant sects. Among the first of these immigrants to arrive was a group of Scottish Presbyterians who settled near Buenos Aires in 1825. By 1826 the congregation had an ordained minister who served there until 1850 (Greenway 1994, 181). Other groups who arrived at various times in the nineteenth century included the Anglican Church of England, the French-speaking Protestant Church, the Waldensian Church (Italian Protestants), the German Evangelical Church, and the Dutch Reform Church (Míguez Bonino 1997, 79–106).

The history of these ethnic Protestant groups has been carefully outlined by Waldo L. Villalpando in his *Las iglesias del transplante: Protestantismo de inmigración en la Argentina* (Transplant churches: Immigrant Protestantism in Argentina, 1970). The author provides a wealth of important historical information; nevertheless, it is interesting to note that the study is carried out with an underlying tone of bias. For instance, Villalpando does not seem willing to consider the fact that Roman Catholicism is also what he terms a "transplant religion." These early Protestant churches differed from late arriving mission Protestant churches, which arrived in Argentina with the goal of increasing church membership by means of conversion. The ethnic Protestants, as minority groups, brought with them and conserved their religion as a means of cultural survival and identity and did not attempt to proselytize.

In the same vein, although not within the context of Protestant religion, one may consider the ethnic religions that African slaves brought with them and preserved in spite of being forced to practice Catholicism outwardly. Slaves secretly organized numerous *cofradías* (brotherhoods or societies) under the watchful eye of the priests and disguised their own African rites among Catholic rituals. The first *cofradía* was established in 1772 in the church La Piedad. The Catholic priests allowed the meetings to take place but they also controlled them carefully. The transculturation of African religion with Catholicism resulted in a unique blend. Two black saints were venerated among the slave population: San Benito and San Baltasar. The Buenos Aires neighborhood of San Telmo was largely populated by Afro-Argentines in the nineteenth century where traditional dancing, music, folk medicine, and religion were commonplace (Coria 1997, 79–88).

In South America, Protestantism has experienced its most wide-reaching impact in Brazil. Studies on the phenomenon of Protestantism, mainly Evangelicalism and Pentecostalism, in Latin America tend to focus on countries like Brazil where it has flourished and spread at an incredible rate. The explanations of why Protestantism has become so popular are multiple, and they include such diverse agendas as the purely political (mainly in the form of cultural invasion from the United States), the medical, the economic, the sociological, the psychological, and the spiritual (Miller 1994). Whatever reasoning one may see as most convincing, and perhaps it is a combination of all of them, the one certainty is that Protestantism is viewed as a menace to Catholicism and to Hispanic identity as they have been traditionally perceived in Latin America. In attempting to unravel the conflictive relationship between Protestantism and Catholicism, David Martin points to the friction between the Hispanic imperium and the Anglo-Saxon imperium which date back 400 years (Martin 1990, 9). This centuries-old strife, which originated on the European continent, has been translated in modern times into a perceived struggle between the predominantly Protestant United States and the overwhelmingly Catholic Latin American countries. More important in considering the Protestant-Catholic relationship, states Martin, are the "dramatically different ways in which Catholic cultures and Protestant cultures have entered into what we call modernity" (1990, 26).

One of the fundamental differences that converts from Catholicism seem to find attractive in Protestantism is the basic organization of the social body. Protestant religions by and large are structured on a sense of community wherein everyone actively participates. In contrast, Catholicism is structured as a hierarchical institution, and in many cases, like in Argentina, it can become associated with authoritarianism. Martin also explains that the single most significant factor contributing to the surge in evangelical Protestantism is the physical migration of massive numbers of people from rural areas to urban centers.

> The new society now emerging in Latin America has to do with movement, and evangelicals constitute a *movement*. Evangelical Christianity is a dramatic migration of the spirit matching and accompanying a dramatic migration of bodies. In undertaking this migration, people become "independent" not at all by building up modest securities but by the reverse: by the loss of all the ties that bind, whether these be familial, communal or ecclesial. Pentecostalism in particular renews these ties in an atmosphere of hope and anticipation rather than of despair. . . . A new faith is able to implant new disciplines, re-order priorities, counter corruption and destructive machismo, and reverse the indifferent and injurious hierarchies of the outside world. Within

this enclosed haven of faith a fraternity can be instituted under firm leadership, which provides for release, for mutuality and warmth, and for the practice of new roles. In this way millions of people are absorbed within a protective social capsule where they acquire new concepts of self and new models of initiative and voluntary organization. (Martin 1990, 284)

In Argentina these large Pentecostal conglomerations have become quite visible within the past ten to fifteen years. Economic constraints, coupled with the sheer numbers of members who attend weekly services, have led to a kind of trend in Argentina—the conversion of defunct movie theaters into church meeting halls. One of the most well-known cinemas in Buenos Aires in now a meeting place for Evangelicals. It is estimated that one third of all regular Sunday church-goers in Buenos Aires belong to some Protestant sect (Wynarczyk 1993, 61).

Very little current information is available on Argentine Protestantism in the form of a comprehensive sociocultural evaluation. Arno W. Enns's 1971 study *Man, Milieu and Mission in Argentina* provides valuable demographic data and information on the presence and growth of ten different sects, including the Mennonites. However, no comparable study has been realized within the past twenty-six years to update that information. In a more popular vein, nevertheless, is Alfredo Silletta's *Las sectas invaden la Argentina* (The sects invade Argentina, 1986). In the seventh edition of the book (1991), Silletta writes that he could never have imagined that his book would become a "classic" among all ages in Argentina and that for him it is "un verdadero orgullo que a siete años de estudiar y denunciar públicamente a las sectas, la gente me asocie a este libro" (a real source of pride that seven years after studying and publicly denouncing sects that people associate this book with me [i]). Silletta's book is decidedly and overtly biased against Protestantism, but it is useful for gaining an understanding of the widespread effect of the phenomenon in Argentina. At any rate, one need not rely solely on gathered statistics to note that the rapid expansion of Protestant religions is beginning to manifest itself in a number of societal ramifications in Argentina, many of which are presented, to varying degrees of credibility, in Silletta's popular pseudo-journalistic book.

Recent figures show that in 1960 Protestants made up 1.63 percent of the total population; by 1985, that number had grown to 4.69 percent. It is estimated that, by the year 2010, 13.6 percent of all Argentines will be Protestant (Stoll 1990, 337). In terms of percentage of population, these figures are low when compared to other Latin American countries. In comparing the cases of Argentina and Chile, David Martin argues that Argentina's Protestant population is much lower than Chile's because of the difference in patterns of immigration. He contends that the Protestant population in Argentina did not grow significantly because it came about as the result of ethnic immigration prior to 1930; in Chile, however, Protestant growth came about as the result of conversion after 1930 and the onset of the economic revolution (1990, 74). Furthermore, Martin argues that historically conversion has been slow to have an effect in Argentina precisely because religion is so strongly tied to ethnic identity, which holds true for Catholics (Creole or immigrant), Protestants, Jews, and one might here add Muslims (75). The success of conversion in Argentina, then, is a relatively recent development. Martin states that the most successful Protestant religions have been the Plymouth Brethren, the Baptists, and the Seventh Day Adventists. He also identifies the emergence of independent charismatic churches such as the Vision of the Future Movement with over 150,000 members as making a "discernible impact" (76).

Argentina has the distinction of being the birthplace of the so-called Billy Graham of Latin America. Luis Palau (b. 1934) came from a working-class family from Ingeniero Maschwitz, a small town in the province of Buenos Aires. He came to the United States as part of a program of Overseas Crusades Ministries to train Latin American religious leaders. He worked for a time as a translator for Billy Graham, married, and received his U.S. citizenship. Palau returned to Latin America where he became successful by utilizing the power of television to promote his message. In many ways, he was an answer to Protestantism's prayers since he delivered North American style with his Latin American personality and image. Palau also met success by playing into the politics of several dictators in power during the 1970s and 1980s throughout Latin America. Palau's strategy was to back the regime publicly in exchange for such benefits as free airtime. Nevertheless, he was often very defensive when accused of promoting right-wing ideologies (Stoll 1990, 121–24). In April 1986 he organized the Festival de la Familia (Festival of the Family), sponsored by the Cruzada de Luis Palau (Luis Palau Crusade), his Oregon-based ministry: 200,000 people packed the Vélez Sarsfield stadium in Buenos Aires (Silletta 1986, 39).

CHURCH OF JESUS CHRIST OF LATTER-DAY SAINTS

The Church of Jesus Christ of Latter-Day Saints is the most prominent Christian, non-Catholic religion in Argentina. Here, one is careful to avoid classifying the Latter-Day Saints—more commonly known as Mormons—as

Protestants since the church and its membership do not identify themselves as Protestants and in fact negate any relationship to Protestant churches and tradition. In terms of total population, Mormons are outnumbered by other, more populist Evangelical and Pentecostal sects. However, they constitute an increasingly noticeable presence within the social makeup of Argentina.

The history of the Mormon church in Argentina began in October 1925 when Melvin J. Ballard, a high-ranking member of the Council of the Twelve Apostles, was instructed to travel to South America to prepare the way for missionary work there. By December of the same year, Ballard and two other officials, Rulon S. Wells and Rey L. Pratt, had arrived in Buenos Aires. One week after arriving, Ballard baptized five people in the Río de la Plata, the first South American Mormons. On December 25, 1925, in an official ceremony held in the Parque 3 de Febrero (part of the lush recreational Palermo park system in Buenos Aires), Ballard "dedicated" Argentina and all of South America for the preaching of church doctrine and the growth of the church. The event, considered to be a milestone in church history, is remembered as an important historical date. Argentina became the headquarters for mission work throughout South America until missions were eventually established in neighboring countries. The first Mormon chapel was completed in Liniers (Province of Buenos Aires) in April 1939.

The rapid growth of the Mormon church in Argentina, as in other parts of the world, is due to the highly organized and efficient missionary program which has taken the church message to 160 nations in 145 languages. Spanish is the second most frequently spoken language in the Mormon church followed by Portuguese. In Argentina there are over 235,000 Mormons who comprise 725 congregations throughout the country. There are now ten separate missions operating in Argentina, the sole function of which is to proselytize. As a result, Argentine membership in the church has more than doubled in the past ten years. Mormon missionaries have become a permanent part of virtually every city and neighborhood in Argentina. They are native Argentines, Americans, or, more rarely, Mormons from other countries. Most missionaries are young men, who typically begin to serve their mission at the age of nineteen. Fewer are women, who may not serve a mission until they are twenty-one years of age. While the vast majority of missionaries are the proselytizing type, there is another category known as welfare missionaries (all women) whose duties revolve around social and educational services similar to those offered by Peace Corps volunteers. Older, retired couples also frequently go on missions, often serving as temple workers. Mormon missionaries do not receive salaries and in fact are responsible for financially supporting themselves during their two-year mission. In recent years, however, the church has restructured the way this is done. It used to be that the family sent their missionary a monthly check based on his or her needs, but there was a considerable disparity given the fact that some missionaries in Latin America needed as little as $150 a month to survive while others in more expensive areas of the world required $500 or more. Families now send a set amount of money to a central missionary fund, and the church issues monthly stipends to its missionaries through the individual mission headquarters. Missionaries or their families who cannot fully support themselves during a mission are aided by the church.

Church members meet regularly on Sundays in their local chapels, but for special ordinances Mormons must attend temples. Prior to the opening of the Buenos Aires temple in 1986, Argentine Mormons had to travel to Brazil or Chile for temple worship. The temple can be seen looming large alongside the highway as one travels into the city center from the Ezeiza International Airport.

Buenos Aires continues to be an important organizational center for the Mormon church as the headquarters for its South America South Area. From here, the church owns and operates a large publishing house which produces scriptures and church materials in Spanish that are distributed throughout the region. Likewise, church business and administration for the region are conducted from the capital.

The success of the Mormon church is a result not only of the hierarchical structuring of the institution but also of the enormous wealth and economic power wielded by the church. Through a system of tithes (all members are expected to give 10 percent of their earnings to the church), as well as income from vast property holdings and investments, the church can afford to build chapels, temples, and schools as well as finance any number of other projects without having to worry about raising money from a small congregation. Also, the only salaried people in the church are those who hold secular jobs, from administrators to janitors. No religious leader receives a salary or financial compensation of any kind. Mission presidents often leave their jobs and sell their homes and other property and move their entire family across the globe in order to fulfill their calling and support themselves throughout the duration of their mission.

The responsibilities of church membership are an enormous part of every aspect of members' lives. Argentine Mormon leaders tend to be middle- to upper-class, well-educated professionals who are financially stable or independent and who are capable of assuming the added responsibility of church leadership in addition to the everyday obligations of their secular lives. Congregations vary according to geographical area, but they typically comprise middle- to lower-class families and individuals. A conspicuous phenomenon within the church, similar to Protestant congregations, is that it attracts a large number of people who live at the poverty level or below.

The Mormon church offers many appealing benefits ranging from welfare aid to a sense of belonging for those who may otherwise feel disenfranchised from the social body and for whom Catholicism offers no tangible benefits. The neatly groomed missionaries in their suits and ties are, if nothing else, a glimpse into a social class that is far removed from their own reality. Missionaries pressured by their president to meet monthly conversion goals and motivated by their own zeal often find easy converts among the extremely poor who are taken in by the outer appearance of the church without ever grasping a real understanding of the complexities of Mormon doctrine. Once baptized these members often become inactive after the novelty of church membership has worn off and the missionaries no longer pay them weekly visits and escort them personally to church on Sundays. However, the average Argentine Mormon is middle-class and maintains a strong connection with the faith and identity as a Mormon. Being a Mormon implies much more than simply belonging to a church. It entails an entire cultural identity and sense of peoplehood that transcend geographic borders and national identities, which grew out of the nineteenth-century beginnings of the Church of Jesus Christ of Latter-Day Saints founded by Joseph Smith.

Mormons have often found it difficult to practice their religion in Argentina. They are the targets of attacks from both the political left and the ultraright. North American Mormon missionaries are often suspected and even accused of being Central Intelligence Agency (CIA) agents. This myth, which is propagated in Silletta's *Las sectas* (1991, 164), stems from reports that the CIA often recruits former Mormon missionaries because they generally exhibit a strong sense of patriotism, observe a strict moral code, and have extensive overseas experience (Heinerman and Shupe 1985, 162–68). Native Argentine missionaries must weather being berated as sellouts to Yankee imperialism among other insults. In October 1976 the Nationalist publication *Cabildo* issued a statement listing Mormons, together with Jews, Jehovah's Witnesses, and others, as subversive threats to the nation (Rock 1992, 227). During the years of the *Proceso*, Mormons were consistently accused of complacence (due mostly to their social status and to the fact that Mormons tend to be politically conservative) or compliance with the dictatorship. Violence against Mormons heightened during the Falkland Islands war (1982) when missionaries lived under the very real threat of being assaulted. Most violence against Mormons is directed at missionaries since they are so readily recognized. Anti-Mormon sentiment in Argentina has never reached the levels of violence that it has in Chile where churches have suffered numerous bomb and arson attacks or in Bolivia where missionaries have been gunned down on the street. Recently (April 1996) two Mormon missionaries were assaulted in Buenos Aires, and one was shot in the back of the head. While this incident probably cannot be linked to any specific politically motivated attack against Mormons, it does make it clear that Mormon missionaries are highly visible targets.

The Mormon presence has reached such a level of recognition in Argentina that it has begun to manifest itself in a variety of ways. For instance, Mormons have begun to appear in literary texts, although they are portrayed negatively. To cite two examples found in a cursory survey, both Rodolfo Enrique Fogwill (1941) and José Luis Najenson (1938) have written stories in which Mormon missionaries are ridiculed and ultimately become the victims of some act of violence. Another illustration of the Mormon permeation into the cultural consciousness can be found in the film *Lo que vendrá* (Times to Come, 1988), directed by Gustavo Mosquera R. The film presents a disturbing apocalyptic vision of oppressive authoritarianism and shows a war-torn, crumbling Buenos Aires. The character played by rock lyricist Charly García follows a corrupt policeman to the outskirts of Buenos Aires where the officer has a chalet, which just happens to be within the vicinity of the Mormon temple. The camera focuses on the temple from a variety of angles and finally zooms in on the figure of the trumpeting angel Moroni that adorns all temples high atop the steeple. One cannot be certain if the close-up of the figure is meant to symbolize an avenging angel (clearly the role the García character sees himself as fulfilling) or one of mercy announcing an era of forthcoming peace. Mosquera most likely found the building useful for its visual effect, but one may also question whether the filmmaker was at the same time attempting to make a statement regarding the popularly alleged conspiratorial relationship between the church and the corrupt government. The point here, nevertheless, remains the same: Mormons have attained a presence, for better or worse, within the cultural landscape of Argentina.

References

Aguinis, Marcos. *Carta esperanzada a un general: puente sobre el abismo.* Buenos Aires: Sudamericana/Planeta, 1983.

———. *La matriz del infierno.* Buenos Aires: Sudamericana, 1997.

———. *Un país de novela: viaje hacia la mentalidad de los argentinos.* Buenos Aires: Planeta, 1988.

Aguinis, Marcos, y Monsignor Justo Laguna. *Diálogos sobre la Argentina y el fin del milenio.* Buenos Aires: Sudamericana, 1996.

Avni, Haim. *Argentina and the Jews: A History of Jewish Immigration.* Trans. by Gila Brand. Tuscaloosa: University of Alabama Press, 1991.

Burdick, Michael A. *For God and the Fatherland: Religion and Politics in Argentina.* Albany: State University of New York Press, 1995.

Comisión Nacional Sobre la Desaparición de Personas. *Nunca más.* 17th ed. Buenos Aires: Eudeba, 1992.

Coria, Juan Carlos. *Pasado y presente de los Negros en Buenos Aires.* Buenos Aires: Editorial Julio A. Roca, 1997.

Dujovne Ortiz, Alicia. *Eva Perón.* Trans. by Shawn Fileds. New York: St. Martin's Press, 1996.

Enns, Arno W. *Man, Milieu and Mission in Argentina.* Grand Rapids, Mich.: William B. Eerdmans Publishing, 1971.

Feierstein, Ricardo. *Contraexilio y mestizaje: ser judío en la Argentina.* Buenos Aires: Milá, 1996.

Greenway, Roger S. "Protestant Missionary Activity in Latin America." In *Coming of Age: Protestantism in Contemporary Latin America,* edited by Daniel R. Miller, 175–204. Lanham, Md.: University Press of America, 1994.

Heinerman, John, and Anson Shupe. *The Mormon Corporate Empire.* Boston: Beacon Press, 1985.

Horovitz, David. "Backlash! Argentina's Jews Face the Bomb's Fallout." *Jerusalem Report* 5, no. 9 (1994): 28–29, 32–35.

Kaufman, Edy, and Beatriz Cymberknopf. "La dimensión judía en la represión durante el gobierno militar en la Argentina." In *El antisemitismo en la Argentina,* edited by Leonardo Senkman, 235–73. 2d ed. Buenos Aires: Centor Editor de América Latina, 1989.

Kovadloff, Santiago. *La nueva ignorancia: Ensayos reunidos.* Buenos Aires: REI Argentina, 1992.

Lockhart, Darrell B., ed. *Jewish Writers of Latin America: A Dictionary.* New York: Garland, 1997.

Martin, David. *Tongues of Fire: The Explosion of Protestantism in Latin America.* Foreword by Peter Berger. Oxford: Basil Blackwell, 1990.

Míguez Bonino, José. *Faces of Latin American Protestantism.* Trans. by Eugene L. Stockwell. Grand Rapids, Mich.: William B. Eerdsman, 1997.

Miller, Daniel R. "Introduction." In *Coming of Age: Protestantism in Contemporary Latin America,* edited by Daniel R. Miller, xiii–xix. Lanham, Md.: University Press of America, 1994.

Mirelman, Víctor A. *En búsqueda de una identidad: los inmigrantes judíos en Buenos Aires, 1890–1930.* Buenos Aires: Milá, 1988.

Official Website of the Church of Jesus Christ of Latter-Day Saints. http:sh/www.lds.org

Rock, David. *Authoritarian Argentina: The Nationalist Movement, Its History and Its Impact.* Berkeley: University of California Press, 1992.

Salinas, Juan José. *AMIA: el atentado. ¿Quiénes son responsables y por qué no están presos?* Buenos Aires: Planeta, 1997.

Shumway, Nicolas. *The Invention of Argentina.* Berkeley: University of California Press, 1991.

Silletta, Alfredo. *Las sectas invaden la Argentina.* Buenos Aires: Puntosur Editores, 1986; 7th ed. 1991.

Siminovich, Javier. "Desaparecidos y antisemitismo en la Argentina, 1976–1983. Las respuestas de la comunidad judía." In *El antisemitismo en la Argentina,* edited by Leonardo Senkman, 310–28. 2d ed. Buenos Aires: Centro Editor de América Latina, 1989.

Stoll, David. *Is Latin America Turning Protestant? The Politics of Evangelical Growth.* Berkeley: University of California Press, 1990.

Taylor, Julie M. *Eva Perón: The Myths of a Woman.* Chicago: University of Chicago Press, 1979.

Timerman, Jacobo. *Prisoner without a Name, Cell without a Number.* Trans. by Toby Talbot. New York: Alfred A. Knopf, 1981.

Villapando, Waldo L. *Las iglesias del transplante: protestantismo de immigración en la Argentina.* Buenos Aires: Centro de Estudios, 1970.

Weisbrot, Robert. *The Jews of Argentina: From the Inquisition to Perón.* Philadelphia: Jewish Publication Society of America, 1979.

Wolff, Martha, and Myrtha Schalom, eds. *Judíos y argentinos: judíos argentinos.* Buenos Aires: Manrique Zago, 1988.

Wynarczyk, Hilario. "Las aproximaciones a la sociología del campo evangélico en la Argentina." In *Ciencias sociales y religión en el Cono Sur,* edited by Alejandro Frigerio, 61–71. Buenos Aires: Centro Editor de América Latina, 1993.

Zago, Manrique, ed. *Pioneros de la Argentina, los inmigrantes judíos* (Pioneers in Argentina, the Jewish immigrants). Buenos Aires: Manrique Zago, 1982.

3

Social Customs

TWO PRINCIPAL FACTORS have led to the decline of a national culture in Argentina in recent years. First, many rituals are changing or even dying out as a result of the neoliberalist economic policies instituted with the return to democracy in 1983. Second, the pervasive influence of American culture has weakened many traditional practices. In spite of these changes, however, there are still many customs that shed light on national characteristics and stem from unique historical circumstances. This chapter describes such unique features with respect to national identity, food and drink, sport, and the celebration of national holidays.

In Argentina, one must be aware of the differences that separate the *Porteños*, or people of the port city and capital of Buenos Aires, who make up nearly 40 percent of the country's total population, from the Argentines in the rest of the country, or the "interior." As a general rule, those of the interior regard the *Porteños* as aggressive, pretentious, high-strung, and loud, while they view themselves as humble, filled with common sense, and more down-to-earth. *Porteños* view their compatriots of the interior as unworldly, ugly, superstitious, and ignorant. They see themselves as attractive, sophisticated, glamorous, and cultured.

That Buenos Aires has the greatest number of residents who have undergone plastic surgery of any city in the entire world reveals much about *Porteño* identity. *Porteños* rarely visit the rest of the country, outside of a few select winter and summer resort spots, preferring whenever economically possible to visit Paris or Miami or simply to stay in Buenos Aires.

While these generalizations relating to the *Porteño* Argentine and the in-

Two businessmen greeting each other in public with a form of physical display common to all social classes as a defiance of the longstanding prudishness enforced by past military regimes. Note that this display does not usually have a sexual connotation. Courtesy of Eduardo Gil.

terior Argentine seem to place them at virtually opposite ends of the spectrum, there are, nonetheless, some characteristics that may be said to bind Argentines as a whole. For example, a melancholy streak tends to run through most Argentines—a sadness and a soul-searching not too common among peoples of other Latin American nations. At the same time, Argentines are also very warm people, something that may be felt quite literally by their extensive physical contact that involves greetings and goodbyes always paired with kissing and hugging. Families tend to be close knit, and children often live with their parents well into adulthood.

While *piropos* (flirtatious comments uttered on the street primarily by men to women) are quite common, they are often spoken almost under the breath or right as the person is passing and within close earshot. Generally, reserve is prized and loud behavior of any sort on the streets is frowned upon (except, it must be noted, as part of the frequent political protests in which Argentines take part). Loud and unusual behavior in general, except at national sporting matches and in protests, is considered to be vulgar.

The Argentine population, which is extremely opinionated, is probably one of the most politically active and impassioned of all Latin Americans. There is an awe-inspiring level of awareness of both national and international topics. However, no matter what the political party or crusade, it will inevitably be contextualized in relation to Peronism. This attests to the tremendous influence of the party and of its most beloved figure, former First Lady Eva Perón, on the people.

Many Argentines were offended by the Andrew Lloyd Webber rock opera, which portrayed Eva Perón as a money-grubbing high-class call girl. Although some protested when rock diva Madonna was cast in the movie role (and managed to charm Peronist President Carlos Menem into allowing the filming of her standing on the balcony of the Casa Rosada in the same spot from which Eva Perón used to speak to her adoring masses in the Plaza de Mayo), they still flocked to the theaters when the film was released in Buenos Aires. Eva Perón remains a revered figure in Argentina, almost sacred, due in large part to being seen as a champion of the poor and the working class whom she referred to as the *descamisados* or "shirtless ones."

Eva in many ways embodied the Argentine preoccupation with fashion. Argentines generally dress quite formally and stylishly compared to Americans and their South American counterparts, and they are always meticulously groomed. A high value is placed on the quality of the article of clothing as opposed to the quantity of articles owned.

Buenos Aires may be one of the few places left in the world where it is common to find women of the upper classes proudly parading about in their expensive fur coats. The ritzy shopping centers of Buenos Aires rival those of Beverly Hills, and residents of the city unable to consume conspicuously will still frequent the centers in order to soak up the ambiance over coffee and a pastry. Perhaps due to the country's Italian legacy and historical ties to cattle raising, leather goods, especially shoes stores, are plentiful, and although they are not inexpensive, the items are of first-rate quality.

Most Argentines are Catholic, and, until recently, it was mandated that the president of the nation be Catholic; all children in Argentina must be registered upon birth with a Christian name. As a child of Syrian immigrants, Argentine President Carlos Menem had to convert to Catholicism before assuming the presidency, in spite of the fact that his ex-wife and daughter are known to be devout Muslims. Divorce in the country was finally legalized in 1987, and abortion remains a hotly contested issue.

In terms of Argentine religiosity, generally the farther one goes from Buenos Aires, the more local versions of Catholicism take on folkloric characteristics and the greater role religion plays in the lives of the people. Pilgrimages are made to local shrines, and offerings are made to unofficial saints. In the northwestern region of Argentina, in festivals such as Carnival, many Christian elements may be seen. It should also be noted that many of the mainstream Protestant sects from the United States have become popular in Argentina, undoubtedly due to the influx of missionaries.

A National Identity Crisis

While Catholicism remains the religion of the majority of residents of the country (see Chapter 2), it does not seem to have much of a hold on the national psyche. "Argentines don't need religion" more than a few *Porteños* have pointed out, "We have Freud." This brings us to another interesting characteristic of the Argentine people: the love of undergoing analysis. There are three times more psychiatrists and psychologists per capita in Buenos Aires than in the entire state of New York, and virtually all middle-class *Porteños* have, at one point or another, undergone psychotherapy. Many theories have attempted to explain this phenomenon. One is that Argentine mental anguish may be attributed to what has been termed the national identity crisis.

Discussing the Argentine identity crisis, ironically, has become an essential characteristic of the Argentine national identity. It is said that Argentines feel confused because they cannot decide if they are Latin Americans or Europeans. They are primarily of European origin and yet they do not form a part of Europe. It has been said that an Argentine is a Spaniard who speaks like an Italian, dresses like a Frenchman, and thinks he is British. Another joke about the Argentine lack of a cohesive identity is that Mexicans descended from the Aztecs, Peruvians descended from the Incas, and Argentines descended from boats. Argentina's immigrant history is heard in its Spanish, spoken with a distinctly Italian lilt and often, at least in Buenos Aires, with a smattering of *lunfardo* and *cocoliche*, two forms of urban slang that borrow heavily from Italian.

The national identity crisis has also been seen as a result of the country's economic decline after having been so promising at the beginning of the century. Whatever the reasons, Freudianism has been a national obsession and is a part of virtually all lives, regardless of class. In fact, the establishment of psychiatric clinics was one of many reforms enacted by Peronism to help members of the workforce.

During the period of the last military dictatorship, the Process of National Reorganization (1976–1983), military authorities viewed the practice of Freudianism as somehow subversive, and books on the topic were removed from shelves and university departments dedicated to the field were shut down or given reduced funding. There is probably no greater way to legitimize something or to incite interest in it than to have it banned by an authoritarian regime. Since the return to democracy, the field has entered yet another period of popularity and shows few signs of diminishing. Within academic circles it has also maintained its popularity in spite of the fact that most international intellectuals have moved on to other theories to explain human behavior.

MATE

Ironically, for a country obsessed with the differences between the *Porteño* and citizens in the interior, it is the rural figure of the gaucho (Argentine nomadic cowboy) who embodies the characteristics deemed specifically unique to the country as a whole. The gaucho has had a significant impact on two of Argentina's greatest passions in terms of food and drink: their love of red meat and *mate*, a green Paraguayan herb that is drunk in a variety of different ways and contains about the same amount of caffeine as a cup of coffee.

One of the most pervasive cultural traits that may be seen almost upon arrival in Argentina is the local consumption of *mate*. To drink *mate* is to engage in the most democratic of Argentine traditions, one that blurs all socioeconomic distinctions and ethnic groups. Argentina is the largest producer and consumer of *mate*, and both the preparation and the consumption of the drink are highly ritualized.

To drink *mate* one needs four things: a hollow gourd, a metal straw called a *bombilla* with a spoonlike strainer at one end (to prevent people from sucking up the tea leaves), the *mate* tea, and hot, but never boiling, water. The host fills the gourd two thirds of the way full with the *mate*, and a bit of cold water is poured in to moisten it. It is then let to stand awhile. Hot water is then poured into the gourd. The *mate* is sucked through the *bombilla* until the water is gone. The gourd is then filled again and passed to the next person in a clockwise direction. Everyone uses the same *bombilla*. The gourd itself can be anything from a plain, hollowed-out squash to a vessel of ornately embellished silver metalwork. The artwork of both *bombillas* and gourds is famous in Argentina, as well as in Uruguay and Brazil.

In Argentina, there are regional differences in the preferred manner of consuming *mate*. In the north of the country, *mate* is normally drunk sweetened, something that annoys *mate* purists, who believe that sugar masks the taste of the leaves and ruins the gourd. It is interesting to note the difference

ch *mate* is drunk in neighboring Uruguay versus Argentina.
much more likely to drink it on the street, carrying thermoses
where they go. This habit is disparaged by the Argentines,
e should be drunk in the home, the "civilized" way. Para-
ile, often enjoy their *mate* ice cold, while Brazilians prefer
to use very large gourds.

Mate is the traditional drink associated with the gaucho, or Argentine cowboy, which brings us back to horsemanship. The gaucho remains one of the best-known cultural symbols of Argentina. He has been elevated to the level of myth in the epic poem *Martín Fierro* by José Hernández and in the novel *Don Segundo Sombra* by Ricardo Güiraldes, and he is celebrated in national culture, considered to embody the most positive attributes of the Argentine individual: strength, bravery, honor, and a fiercely independent spirit.

THE GAUCHO

The existence of the figure itself remains the subject of debate. Much like the American cowboy, some say that the "real" gaucho disappeared in the late nineteenth century when he was robbed of his independent and self-sustaining life by being forced to become a hired hand on large ranches. Others feel that the gaucho survives today in the spirit of the men whose lives are still tied to cattle raising and horsemanship, in spite of the radical changes his world has undergone.

There is some agreement that the gauchos first came into being on what is today part of the territory of Uruguay. The first gauchos were mostly mestizos, of mixed Spanish and indigenous blood. Cattle and horses that had escaped from the Spanish settlements roamed the Pampas, and the gauchos caught and tamed the horses and then used them to capture cattle. Interestingly enough, the primary value of the cattle was the hides they provided, a source of clothing and warmth, and not the meat.

The first gauchos lived by selling hides for tobacco, rum, and *mate*. Gauchos were said to be so addicted to *mate* that if given a choice between beef and *mate, mate* would win every time. The gauchos lived with few possessions, just a horse, saddle, poncho, and knife, and they spent their free time drinking and gambling in saloons. This deadly combination led to the emergence of another favorite gaucho pastime, knife fights. The elaborately decorated gaucho knife, the *facón*, remains a symbol of Argentine craftsmanship. The primary reputation of the gaucho, however, continues to be for his skill with horses.

It has been said that the gaucho and his horse were inseparable, almost one being, and that a gaucho without his horse was like a man without his legs. Almost all of the daily chores were done on horseback. The first gauchos hunted with *boleadoras*, three leather-wrapped stones or metal balls attached to the ends of connected ropes. The gauchos threw the *boleadoras* at just the right angle to trip fleeing cattle. The emphasis on horsemanship among the gauchos eventually led to organized competitions.

One of the more famous events is called the *sortija*, in which the horseman rides as fast as possible with a lance in his hand to catch a ring dangling from a crossbar. Another competition is the *marona*, in which the gaucho drops from the corral gate while a herd of wild horses is driven out beneath him. He must use all his strength to land on a horse's back, control it, and return it to the gate. In the *piliar*, the horseman rides through a gauntlet of partners who, using lassos, attempt to trip the horse. The object of the competition is for the gaucho to land on his feet with the reins still in his hand.

The clothing of the gaucho is a source of pride. The gauchos wore the *chiripá*, a diaperlike cloth draped between the legs which was suitable for riding. This was later replaced by the *bombachas*, loose-fitting pants. Around his waist the gaucho wore a *faja*, or woolen sash, and a *rastra*, a stiff, wide leather belt adorned with coins. The *facón*, the gaucho's knife, was his most prized possession after his horse. The knife was used throughout the day for skinning, self-defense, and eating. The outfit was completed with a bright kerchief tied around the neck, spurs, and a vest. The poncho, worn over the outfit, served also as a blanket at night.

While the traditional gaucho is said to have become extinct by the late nineteenth century, there is still much of the culture that remains. The competitions between horsemen still go on, and the traditional outfit is worn with pride at such events. When the tango became the rage in Europe during the 1930s, one of the strangest sights was the mistaken appropriation of gaucho attire for dance shows in Europe, in an attempt to exoticize for Europeans a dance that was essentially an Argentine urban phenomenon.

Related to the cattle-raising tradition of the gaucho and the country's historical economic dependence on livestock is the country's considerable consumption of red meat. Most national dishes are based on the plentiful supply of beef that may be broiled, grilled, fried, or boiled and is eaten at least once a day and sometimes twice. The great promise of the Argentine economy during the last century stemmed in large part from the development at the end of the 1800s of ways of chilling and storing meat. At this time, Argentine beef began crossing the Atlantic regularly.

The economy boomed, and railways were built by the British in part to

Tango dancers at a street fair. Courtesy of Eduardo Gil.

serve the tremendous demand for bringing the beef from the countryside to the ports to ship it to Europe. The wealthiest families in Buenos Aires sent their offspring to Europe with Argentine cows in tow to make sure they would eat only the finest beef. Today one of the prevailing traditions in Argentina is that of the *parrillada* or grill on Saturday afternoons with the entire family. Argentines consider the weekly, if not daily, consumption of a good steak to be their birthright, and they are justifiably proud and anxious to share this national passion with visitors.

Also related to the country's cattle past is the yearly festival La Rural, held in July in Buenos Aires. It may be considered the rough equivalent of a state fair, only it is given for Argentina's cattle-raising high society. During the weeks of La Rural, livestock are brought into the capital from all over the country for competitions. Artwork from each of the country's regions, as well as from other parts of the world, is on display. The president of the nation traditionally appears at La Rural, and there are competitions to demonstrate horsemanship skills daily in an arena at the center of the fairgrounds, an elegant version of a rodeo. One of the more delicious ways to experience the world-famous Argentine meat is the *empanada*, a pielike bread filled with meat.

OTHER TRADITIONAL FOODS

Empanadas are common throughout the Southern Cone region, with differences from country to country in size and fillings. In Argentina they are generally stuffed with beef, ham and cheese, hard-boiled eggs, vegetables, or other fillings and served warm. *Empanadas* may be spicy or bland and may be baked or fried. They are a staple in the Argentine diet, cheap and plentiful.

Argentina's love for beef has continued despite the appearance of vegetarian restaurants and nasty medical predictions for those who continue to eat red meat. It also has withstood the economic hardships that have forced many families to reduce their consumption of beef during the last ten years. Argentines remain devoted to their beef; it is seen as a measure of prosperity in a very prosperity-conscious country. Per capita consumption of beef is 220 pounds per year, compared to 78 pounds in the United States. On those occasions when Argentines are unable to buy meat, they often eat a favorite dish related to the country's Italian legacy, *ñoquis*.

Ñoquis are potato dumplings served with a marinara or white sauce and occasionally with meatballs. They are inevitably the cheapest item on a menu and are considered to be poor-man's fare. One tradition related to the dish is the eating of *ñoquis* on the twenty-ninth of every month. The idea is that by the end of the month family funds have run so low that *ñoquis* are the only thing left that the family can afford to eat. However, a peso will be placed under each plate to save face, as a way of saying that there really is at least a bit of money left and that the *ñoquis* are eaten by choice and tradition rather than necessity. The coin is also seen as the harbinger of good fortune. This again reflects the prosperity-conscious side of the Argentines. Argentine cuisine is very heavily influenced by its Italian immigrant roots, and some of the best pizzas in the world may be found in the country, and a variety of pasta dishes and sauces are available in most "Argentine" restaurants.

BRITISH INFLUENCE

Several traditions stem from the country's historical ties to England. The British influence is still widely felt in Argentina, especially in Buenos Aires. For example, there is still a clearly British-inspired changing of the guard in the city at the government house. In the nineteenth century and into the twentieth century, Britons owned and managed the country's gas, water, and telephone systems. Railways were designed by British engineers and financed by British bankers with the intent of getting beef from the interior to the ports as soon as possible. There has also historically been a large British population in Buenos Aires.

Due to the British legacy in Argentina, tea time is still observed, though much less so than in the past. The tea houses in Buenos Aires are some of the most strikingly beautiful edifices in the city and retain a turn-of-the-century charm. One can still go to such tea rooms as the Richmond, the old haunt of Argentina's most celebrated author, Jorge Luis Borges, and enjoy the ritual of tea and scones at five o'clock daily.

Quite literally at the center of many Argentine pastries and desserts is *dulce de leche*, a soft caramel that Argentines adore and use much in the way peanut butter is used in the United States. It may be spread on bread, crackers, or fruit, rolled in a pastry, or a tucked into a cone resembling a Cuban cigar and sold by packs of five on the street as *cubanitos* (little Cubans). *Dulce de leche* is also the ubiquitous middle layer (occasionally chocolate instead) of an *alfajor*, the perennial Argentine snack of two sandwiched cookies dipped in white or dark chocolate. Among the most expensive of the *alfajor* brands is Havana, considered by many Argentines to be the most delectable. A yellow six-pack-box of Havana *alfajores* is the ultimate treat to take to an Argentine living abroad. The Havana stores located throughout the country sell boxes of *alfajores* and canisters of *dulce de leche*. Argentine pastries rival those of the French. It is virtually impossible to continue walking down a street when faced with an alluring display of colorful tiny cakes and pies in a bakery window, ready to be carefully wrapped in paper, tied with a colorful ribbon, and taken home and eaten while drinking *mate* or sipping tea.

CAFÉS

Argentina's love of sweet confections and talking may be seen as a cause or effect of their lively café life. Social life and to a great extent business life revolve around the cafés of the capital called *confiterías* (confectioneries). There are cafés on virtually every corner of the city, many of them elegant and refined, such as the historic Tortoni or El Molino, which retain their turn-of-the-century charm. Others are quite modest or are modern facilities of glass and chrome.

Buenos Aires's café society is of paramount importance to most residents, and it rivals those of Paris and Rome. The rise of the society may be seen as possibly a response to the need to have a meeting place outside of the home, possibly from the immigrant history of the country that led many lonely men to look for companionship. The early cafés were primarily the reserve of men, although later *salónes de familia* (family salons), where women could go to meet each other, were opened.

In Buenos Aires, *Porteños* feel a deep sense of loyalty to their café. In fact, many cafés have become known for the interests of the people who patronize the establishment. Thus, one may inquire which literary, political, student, artistic, or social group frequents a particular café. Virtually every important event to take place in Argentine history has been discussed at length in the city's *confiterías*, and many literary works and tangos use them as their setting. During the military dictatorship of 1976–1983, the police often raided the *confiterías* known to be frequented by those who opposed the government, and it was common for the government regularly to plant infiltrators in the café crowds in order to monitor activities and discussions.

One of the more interesting demonstrations of the high level of Argentine intellectual activity is the *taller literario* or literary workshop. A writer who has achieved some measure of fame may advertise the workshop in the paper, and aspiring writers join and meet weekly in an attempt to fine-tune their own skills. The literary workshops in many ways are the Argentine version of the extended university, only they are not formally monitored by any institution. Many of the country's most famous writers have both attended and given literary workshops, and the income generated by doing so is important in a country where writers make little money.

NIGHTLIFE

Many *talleres literarios* revolve around the work of aspiring playwrights, revealing the great love of theater shared by most *Porteños*. Buenos Aires has a very developed night life, one that has withstood the dictatorships of the 1970s and the economic pressures of the 1980s and 1990s, and it continues to thrive. A comparison can be made between the nightlife of Buenos Aires and that of New York City, where shops, restaurants, and bars that cater to the young are open all night. It is said that one may go to the theater virtually every night for a month and not repeat a performance in Buenos Aires.

Buenos Aires remains also one of the safest cities in Latin America, and it is possible to walk the streets at any hour, regardless of age or sex, and feel safe. There is, however, one segment of the population that does have a slightly higher risk of injury in Argentina (as in most countries): the gay male population still is occasionally subjected to gay bashing.

In Buenos Aires, nightlife is so pervasive that many do not even begin their evenings until past midnight. Often times, one can find performances beginning at 2 A.M. Corrientes Avenue is referred to as the "street that never sleeps" or the "Broadway of Buenos Aires." However, unlike Broadway in New York City the ambiance on Corrientes is exceedingly intellectual. Bookstores, found everywhere, are open past midnight, some all night. There are theaters, a cultural center, plenty of international films, and cafés. The evening usually starts late and ends at dawn, long after the buses have stopped running.

Incidentally, Argentines insist that they invented the bus service. The *colectivo* in Buenos Aires conjures up a particular kind of bus, one unique to the city, almost cartoonlike in appearance with often garish color combinations marking their particular route. They run throughout the city and are usually jam-packed at rush hour.

SPORTS

Soccer

It is virtually impossible to discuss Argentina, or Latin America at all, without discussing the popularity of soccer. Soccer, like the consumption of *mate*, may be said to be a unifying factor that transcends class, wealth, and status. Everyone watches soccer and is thrilled by the matches. In Buenos Aires, the tradition is for the fans of the winning team to celebrate at the city's most prominent monument, the Obelisk. On Sunday afternoons men get together to play on the fields and empty lots and everyday, wherever a patch of land is seen, children may be found kicking around a soccer ball. Another reason that the game may be so popular is that it offers the chance for citizens to watch something in which rules *are* followed, in which those who play unfairly are given their just retribution, and all are following the same rules without exceptions. This is often a far cry from the way things are run in other aspects of daily life.

Soccer has had a tremendous effect on all of the countries of the Southern Cone, and players often play their peak years in Europe. After dominating Olympic soccer in the 1920s, Uruguay won the World Cup twice (1930,

The Buenos Aires obelisk, which marks the site of the first raising of the Argentine flag of independence. The obelisk, the symbol of the city, is situated in the middle of the Avenida 9 de Julio, the broadest avenue of the Americas. Courtesy of Eduardo Gil.

1950) and Argentina won in 1978 and 1986 and finished second in 1990. Countries have also sought to increase international prestige by hosting tournaments. The World Cup was hosted by Uruguay in 1930, by Chile in 1962, and by Argentina in 1978. Some critics, however, were repulsed by the way in which Argentina staged an elaborate event during one of the most brutal periods of repression in its history. The 1978 World Cup in Argentina was seen by many to be an attempt to avert the attention of the world from the military's apalling record of human rights.

During important soccer matches, especially during the World Cup, the streets of major cities are deserted, the restaurants are quiet, and there is an eery silence punctured by fits of shouting. People are huddled around televisions and radios following the latest moves of their players. Every match commands undivided attention, and victories are cause for unparalleled celebration. When Argentina won the World Cup in 1986, hundreds of

Boys playing soccer in a city plaza, one of the favorite male sports of the city. Courtesy of Eduardo Gil.

thousands of people flooded the streets of Buenos Aires, Córdoba, Rosario, La Plata, and every other major city. Parades appeared out of nowhere with cars jamming into the streets, horns blaring wildly, and everyone and everything decked out in blue and white (Argentina's national colors).

Soccer was first introduced to Argentina in the 1860s by British sailors who used it as a way to pass the time when the ships were docked. In 1891 Argentina's British community organized the first official game and imported all of the accoutrements such as balls, nets, and goalposts from Europe. By the turn of the century, the sport had officially caught on and Argentina established its own soccer league. The first World Cup in which Argentina participated was held in neighboring Uruguay in 1930. Argentina came in second, after the host country. Soccer became a national sport in 1931. The two most popular teams are River Plate and Boca Juniors, and the majority of the Argentines express allegiance to one or the other.

The enthusiasm exhibited at soccer games makes American sports fans look somewhat indifferent. It has actually reached dangerous proportions in recent years, and as a result new fences have been built and armed guards hired to keep rival fans away from each other and away from the players and umpires.

The love for the game has led to some unusual situations. For example, when Diego Maradona threatened to leave his team to compete in Europe in 1982, the government attempted to intervene by declaring him to be "national patrimony" and thus making his participation in other countries illegal. The attempt failed, and Maradona left for Europe. Although there is considerable talent in terms of the athletes in South America, few countries can offer as much of a financial incentive to their players as can the clubs of England, Spain, and Italy, and so it is very common for players to play elsewhere.

Pato

Pato, another sport that is popular in Argentina, originated in the countryside. It is a cross between basketball and polo. The earliest references to the game date from virtually the founding of the country in the seventeenth century. *Pato*, which means "duck" in Spanish, was originally played with an unfortunate live duck in a basket that had handles on it and two teams of horsemen. The teams would compete to see who could get the duck and return to their settlement. The only hard-and-fast rule was that the horseman with the duck had to keep it extended in his right hand, which inevitably led to a tug-of-war between the players in which one would be dragged off his horse and occasionally trampled to death.

Pato was banned by the government in 1822, but it was resurrected in 1937. At one point, the Catholic Church excommunicated anyone caught playing the game. A set of rules was drawn up to refine the game, which included no longer using a live duck, but rather a ball which must be thrown through a basket located on either end of a field.

Celebration

No sporting celebration would be complete without the obligatory pilgrimage to the city center of Buenos Aires to the Obelisk of the champions. Celebrants dance around the plaza in front of the monument, music blaring, horns blowing, flags waving; and a procession of cars carrying fans parades up and down the 9 de Julio Avenue. One of the more interesting celebrations occurred after Brazil won the World Cup in soccer in July 1994 after defeating Italy. Surprisingly enough, for a country of so many Italian descen-

Madres de la Plaza de Mayo (Plaza de Mayo Mothers) gather, each Thursday, as they have since the 1970s, to demand information on their children who were "disappeared" by the neofascist military governments 1976–1983. Courtesy of Eduardo Gil.

dants, Argentina by and large was rooting for their South American neighbor, and the city erupted in celebration after the Brazilians won.

DEMONSTRATIONS

The mood of that Sunday evening was contagious, but, in retrospect, the innocence in all that gaiety was lost forever the following morning when Argentina experienced its worst terrorist attack ever, the car bombing of the building of the Asociación Mutual Israelita Argentina (AMIA) downtown. The bomb caused eighty-six deaths and became one of the most sorrowful *Porteño* traditions, which is maintained to this day—the gathering each Monday morning in front of the Tribunales courts of various groups from the Jewish community to demand that those guilty of the atrocity be found and brought to justice. Since the bombing of the AMIA and the earlier bombing of the Israeli embassy, the Argentine Jewish community has heavily fortified its synagogues, schools, and cultural centers.

The Monday demonstrations echo the demonstrations that have taken place every Thursday for the last twenty years: the silent protests of the Mothers and Grandmothers of the Plaza de Mayo. These women continue to circle the city square in front of the presidential palace, the Casa Rosada, wearing their white kerchiefs that have become the symbol of mothers around the world and their fight to learn the whereabouts of their missing children taken during the so-called Argentine Dirty War that took place between 1976 and 1983.

HOLIDAYS AND HOLY DAYS

Argentines have an odd relationship to death, one that led novelist Tomás Eloy Martínez to describe them as "cadaver cultists." He explains that they honor their most beloved national figures not on the day of their birth but on the day of their death. Flag Day, for example, takes place on the day that the designer of Argentina's flag, Manuel Belgrano, died, and schoolchildren often learn by heart the dying words of national leaders.

The Recoleta cemetery in Buenos Aires may be said to embody this odd national obsession. The wealthy dead are housed in ornate familial mausoleums, each with its own architectural style. Eva Perón rests in the Recoleta, although her body went on its own world tour after her death, traveling first to Italy and then to Spain where her husband lived in exile, before returning to Buenos Aires. Chacarita, a down-scale version of La Recoleta, nonetheless houses its own celebrities, among them the tango star beloved by all Argentines, Carlos Gardel. Gardel died in 1935, and yet many continue to make a pilgrimage to his tomb to place a fresh flower in the lapel of the life-size statue of him located on the site. On the anniversary of Gardel's death, June 26, many Argentines make the trip to his tomb, and cars are backed up for miles on the streets leading to the cemetery. These annual pilgrimages take on an almost festive air, which leads us to discuss Argentine peculiarities on other, more traditional holidays.

Argentines celebrate Christmas and the Holy Week with all the typical components originally brought from Europe. What is unusual is that these holidays are out of sync seasonally because the Southern Hemisphere has the opposite seasons of the Northern Hemisphere. Thus, Easter, traditionally associated with spring, is celebrated in Argentina during autumn. The very wintery holiday of Christmas falls in the middle of summer, and yet the traditional foods, meant to warm one on a snowy winter's day, are still served. Sweating Santas may also be seen on city streets, dressed in complete Santa Claus regalia despite the heat.

Other holidays celebrated include Day of the Nation, on November 10,

The Recoleta, the "city of the dead" cemetery, in fashionable Barrio Norte in Buenos Aires. Both Juan Domingo Perón and Eva Duarte de Perón are buried here (in separate mausoleums), as well as many of the most prominent figures in Argentine social, political, and cultural history. Courtesy of Eduardo Gil.

in which gauchos parade along the streets of towns throughout the country. On December 30, there is a ticker-tape parade downtown (not on December 31, as is traditional elsewhere, because all offices are closed). Office workers throw their calendars and other paper products out from high-rise buildings and passersby on the street stuff streamers into car and bus windows. One of the most important fairs celebrated each year is the International Book Fair, South America's largest, an event that in Argentina regularly attracts more than a million visitors. Argentines are well known for being among the most literate and intellectual of all South Americans, and the book fair plays a prominent role in demonstrating this to the world.

The traditions that are maintained provide a glimpse into the rich history of each nation and its inhabitants. It is to be hoped that in spite of the rapid changes taking place, which have blurred distinctions among countries and peoples, there will always remain a legacy from the past that will reflect, on a national level, the characteristics and rituals of each country.

A view of the financial district of Buenos Aires from Puerto Madero, an old port area that has recently been renovated for leisure activities as part of current neoliberalism. Courtesy of Eduardo Gil.

REFERENCES

El Ateneo: biografías, historia, geografía y cultura de la República Argentina. CD-ROM. Buenos Aires: Universal Soft, 1997.

Ball, Deirdre. "Wild Orphans of La Pampa." In *Insight Guides Argentina,* edited by Deirdre Ball, 285–90. Singapore: APA Publications, 1988.

Boroughs, Don. "The Pampa." In *Buenos Aires Insight City Guides,* edited by Kathleen Wheaton, 199–201. Singapore: APA Publications, 1988.

Box, Ben, ed. *South American Handbook.* Chicago: Passport Books, 1996.

Evans, Judith. "Meet Me at the Café." In *Buenos Aires Insight City Guides,* edited by Kathleen Wheaton, 119–21. Singapore: APA Publications, 1988.

Foster, Derrick H. N. "Beef and Wines of Argentina." In *Buenos Aires Insight City Guides,* edited by Kathleen Wheaton, 116. Singapore: APA, Publications, 1988.

———. "Eating Out in Buenos Aires." In *Buenos Aires Insight City Guides,* edited by Kathleen Wheaton. 115. Singapore: APA Publications, 1988.

———. "Mate: Argentina's National Drink." In *Buenos Aires Insight City Guides,* edited by Kathleen Wheaton, 144–46. Singapore: APA Publications, 1988.

Gowar, Rex P. "Football." In *Buenos Aires Insight City Guides,* edited by Kathleen Wheaton, 115. Singapore: APA Publications, 1988.

Perrottet, Anthony. "A Night at the Opera." In *Buenos Aires Insight City Guides,* edited by Kathleen Wheaton, 124–26. Singapore: APA Publications, 1988.

Ross, Stanley R., and Thomas F. McGann. *Buenos Aires: 400 Years.* Austin: University of Texas Press, 1982.

Weil, Eric. "Polo and Pato." In *Buenos Aires Insight City Guides,* edited by Kathleen Wheaton, 186–92. Singapore: APA Publications, 1988.

———. "Snacking." In *Buenos Aires Insight City Guides,* edited by Kathleen Wheaton, 142. Singapore: APA Publications, 1988.

4

Broadcasting and Print Media

PRINT MEDIA

IT IS SAID that the history of newspapers in Buenos Aires began in the year 1810, on Thursday, June 7. It was at that time that *La Gazeta de Buenos Ayres*, launched by Mariano Moreno, first came into circulation. The slogan of the new paper was, "It is a rare happiness when there are times in which one is able to feel what one likes and say what one feels" (Ulanovsky 1997, 13). Moreno felt it was crucial that the newspaper transmit to the people the composition of the new organization of power in the country as well as the ideals embodied in the concepts of independence, equality, and freedom.

Between the years 1810 and 1820, in the River Plate region, over 100 newspapers went in and out of circulation. From 1810 to 1870 the journalism that evolved in the country was tied to politics and generally represented the interests of one group or another. Journalists, in fact, were regarded primarily as politicians until 1867 when a new newspaper was founded, *La Capital*, in the city of Rosario. In *La Capital* topics of general interest as well as the daily news were reported, and the newspaper was one of the first to present diverse opinions on its pages. Granted, the inception of the paper and its name had to do specifically with the goals of Ovidio Lagos who desperately wanted the capital of the country to be placed in his city in the interior and not in the port city of Buenos Aires.

Manuel Bilbao, a Chilean living in Argentina, who founded his newspaper *La República* in 1873, decided to try a new approach—let young boys go out and sell the papers in the streets. It was a tremendously novel idea. Prior to this, newspapers were distributed only to subscribers, and oftentimes the only way to get a copy was to go to the newspaper office. To sell a newspaper by shouting in the street was considered a vulgar proposition; nevertheless, it caught on quickly.

Perhaps because of the political nature of the country's early newspapers, many journalists later became statesmen, including Bartolomé Mitre and Domingo Faustino Sarmiento, two of Argentina's forefathers. When Sarmiento became president of the country in 1868 he was not only an active journalist, he believed that one was able to exercise power via the newspapers. "The newspaper," according to Sarmiento, "is for modern people what the Forums were to the Romans" (Ulanovsky 1997, 17).

Between October 1869 and January 1870, in a period of only four months, two giants among newspapers, *La Prensa* and *La Nación*, emerged. The country's first census had been conducted under the direction of Sarmiento, and it was determined that over one third of the country's citizens (a population of 1,877,000) were able to read and write. In the first year of the twentieth century, *La Prensa* reached an unprecedented circulation of 100,000 in Buenos Aires (Ulanovsky 1997, 18).

It was the ex-president of the republic, Bartolomé Mitre, who was the driving force behind *La Nación* when it began circulation in January 1870. The purpose that Mitre had in mind was the consolidation of national identity by way of the paper. On the pages of *La Nación* citizens were able to read about commercial activities of the port and customs information, both crucially important to a city dependent upon maritime commerce.

In *La Prensa*, citizens had access not only to information about the arrival and departure of ships but also about stocks and the activities of the Catholic Church. *La Prensa* soon had sections devoted to literature, primarily texts connected to the formation of the Argentine national identity, such as stories about gauchos. Gradually both papers began to expand their coverage of international events. *La Nación* began to send out correspondents around the country and even abroad. It was Mitre with *La Nación* who found a place in his paper for the advertisements of products. The study of these early advertisements is in many ways as informative of the times as the information provided in the news columns and headlines.

Soon other newspapers began to spring up both in Buenos Aires and around the country. *El Diario*, founded in 1881 by the educator Manuel Lainez, became an important paper in the capital. In Mendoza, in 1882, *Los Andes* was launched, and in La Plata, in 1884, *El Día* was founded. In 1885 two future presidents, Carlos Pellegrini and Roque Sáenz Peña, took over the direction of the newspaper *Sudamérica*. Finally, in 1894, *Los Principios* was founded in Córdoba.

While these newspapers were on the rise, other papers, devoted to humor, emerged. Humor journals such as *El Mosquito* (1863–1893) formed an important part in the emerging national identity. *El Mosquito* allowed a reader to laugh about politicians, the railway system, and government projects that had ended in failure. *El Mosquito* also carried a substantial section featuring cartoons. The French cartoonist Henri Stein was considered the most talented cartoonist of the day, and even Sarmiento wanted to make certain that his image would be drawn by Stein and used in the paper (Ulanovsky 1997, 23).

Caras y Caretas was an important magazine for its popularity and for its combination of four fundamental components: humor, literature, art, and current events. It was founded in October 1898 under the direction of José S. Alvarez ("Fray Mocho"). With the biting humor conveyed through the drawings of Manuel Mayol (Ulanovsky 1997, 24), *Caras y Caretas* became the most important early magazine in the country's history and a mainstay in most households for the next four decades. The magazine was directed at a general public, and there was something in it for all tastes. Generally each edition contained fiction and poetry, photographs of current events and personalities, cartoons, humorous essays, caricatures, and, as Howard Fraser has noted, "the finest multi-color printing of the day" (Fraser 1987, 2). It was on the pages of *Caras y Caretas* that Argentines first voiced the opinion that their city was the "Paris" of South America.

On September 15, 1876, the first *Buenos Aires Herald* appeared, a weekly paper written for members of the British community living in Buenos Aires. The newspaper was dedicated to keeping the citizens aware of the commercial happenings in the port. In 1878 the paper also began to deal with topics of general interest. The newspaper, still in circulation to this day, has generally been known for its serious approach to all issues. During the fierce military repression of the 1970s and early 1980s, the *Buenos Aires Herald* openly condemned military use of violence and torture. The editor received so many death threats that he had to go into exile with his family to avoid detention.

Other than *Caras y Caretas*, the most important magazine founded in Buenos Aires was *El Hogar Argentino*, which was first printed in 1904. The magazine, directed at the emerging middle class, offered advice to women on family matters and suggestions to men about the authors and books they should be reading and tastes they should be cultivating. The magazine provided its readers insight into the world of the upper class. This fascination with the lives of members of the wealthy community was eventually replaced by a devotion to the screen and radio stars who emerged in the 1930s and 1940s.

It must be noted that Argentina was one of the first countries in the world to pass a law concerning the right of citizens to education in 1884. Thus, a tremendous reading public eagerly snatched up journals and magazines as fast as they appeared, so much so that in 1926, Argentines were the consumers of some 66 percent of all newspapers that circulated in Latin America (Ulanovsky 1997, 35). This changed when radio and television emerged, offering competition to the newspapers although many of the newspaper owners were quick to jump into the radio market and establish their own stations.

It was on November 12, 1920, that the newspaper *La Nación* published for the first time photographs that had been taken the day before. The event photographed had occurred some 500 kilometers from the capital in Paraná and the film was transported by plane to Buenos Aires to be developed and ready for distribution the next day. By 1928 the circulation of *La Nación* had grown to 300,000.

The growing power of the newspapers in Buenos Aires was made apparent throughout this century by virtue of the numerous times that newspaper offices, editors, and journalists were directly involved in the events of the day. In other words, they were not just reporting the news; they were often making it. It has been said, for example, that the newspaper *La Crítica* helped bring down the presidency of Hipólito Yrigoyen. The day that the government of Yrigoyen fell the newspaper circulation soared to 1 million copies. It was hardly surprising to many when the new president, José Félix Uriburu, imprisoned the paper's director, Natalio Botano (Ulanovsky 1997, 44). It was *La Crítica*, in the 1930s, that was the first Argentine newspaper to ever reach a circulation of 1 million copies in one day.

Another example of a newspaper making news can be found when, in 1939, rumors were circulating that the president of the nation, Roberto Ortiz, was blind. Félix Laiño, from the paper *La Razón*, asked for a private interview with Ortiz. While pretending to trip, Laiño disturbed ever so slightly the path along which the president was supposed to walk. He was able to ascertain immediately that the president was, indeed, blind, and the following day he wrote an editorial that called into question Ortiz's capacity to lead the country. The editorial provoked a crisis in Argentina and the eventual resignation of the president himself.

Not surprisingly, with these sorts of antics, in the 1930s and 1940s, as confirmed by Tomás Eloy Martínez, the profession of journalism became somewhat disreputable. It was not until 1960, according to Martínez, that journalism once again regained some of its dignity (Ulanovsky 1997, 47). In the 1930s, some magazines were devoted to the emerging radio, film, and theater stars. The literary journal *Sur* began to be published then as well, the result of an entire team of writers under the direction of a wealthy intellectual, Victoria Ocampo.

The focus in *Sur* was on intellectual debates related to aesthetics, not to politics, a marked change in the country. Although many criticized the magazine's reverence for European tastes and dismissed it as elitist, it was a way for some of the most important texts and authors within the country to become known.

During World War II paper was scarce, and all of the newspapers and magazines were forced to cut the number of pages that would be produced in each edition as well as the general circulation. It was at this time that the habit of borrowing a neighbor's newspaper developed in Argentina. Many members of the press were trying to influence the country to depart from its stance of neutrality in the war, and in a period of growing unease the president of the country, Ramón S. Castillo, decided to declare a state of siege. He suspended the constitution and censored the press. Three other events were to have a significant impact during the 1940s in the realm of journalism: (1) the death of Roberto Arlt, a famous journalist for *El Mundo* and writer of the "Aguafuertes," short essays that reflected upon life in Buenos Aires; (2) the ascent of Juan Perón to power in the mid-1940s; and (3) the launching of what would become one of the country's most important papers, *Clarín*, in 1945 by Roberto Noble.

For *Clarín*'s first run, 150,000 copies were printed, and these were given out for free. The price of *Clarín* was five pesos, half the price of the other major newspapers of the day. Each edition had twenty pages, one of which reported sports and two of which discussed performing arts events in the city. From 1945 to 1950, the slogan of the newspaper was, "Argentine solutions to Argentine problems," and the popularity and circulation of the newspaper rose rapidly. It arrived on the streets before all of the other major papers each morning.

Perón was not quick to grasp the popularity of the newspaper and he exerted little control over it initially, allowing journalists for the most part to publish what they wanted. When Perón finally realized the value of the press, he was quick to act. He suspended any papers or magazines that printed any opinions against Peronism, and he established his own press offices that distributed only what he wanted. In 1946, when he assumed the presidency, only one newspaper, *La Época*, supported him. By the time the military overthrew him in 1955, he controlled many more.

Between 1943 and 1946, 110 publications in the country were forced to close, although many simply continued to publish underground. In 1949, when *La Nación* published information about the torture of those who opposed Peronism, the government forces immediately went to work to make it nearly impossible for the paper to continue to be published. They subjected the offices to bogus inspections in an effort to find justification for closing it down, and they attempted to curtail the connection between the newspapers and those who provided them with paper. Official radio programs were established to refute the daily editorials that emerged on the pages of *La Prensa* and *La Nación*.

In 1951 Perón's patience with *La Prensa* ran out. It was decided that the newspaper, the most prestigious one in the city with the highest circulation and the one considered by many to be the most credible, was shut down. The newspaper reappeared later in the year under a new pro-Perón directorship. The effect this event had on the other papers was chilling. Self-censorship became common. *Clarín* and *La Nación* were more cautious than ever.

It was in 1996 that Tomás Eloy Martínez recalled that Perón would undoubtedly have refused to acknowledge what he had done to *La Prensa*, offering what he felt could have been a plausible Peronist counterargument. Perón was not trying to criticize the press but rather he had felt the need to "help" out when it looked as though certain newspapers were going bankrupt (Ulanovsky 1997, 95). From 1951 to 1955, the readership of *La Prensa* in its new guise plummeted. Meanwhile, *Clarín* benefited by gaining a whole new reading public.

On June 16, 1955, members of the Argentine navy and the air force, who had decided to get rid of Perón, bombed the government palace in an effort to kill him. Instead, however, nearly 300 people in the Plaza de Mayo, all unarmed civilians, were massacred. By September of that year Peronism officially ended, and the leader was forced into exile in Spain. At the time Perón controlled seventeen newspapers, ten journals, four information agencies, more than forty radio channels, and the only television station in the country.

The eighteen years of Perón's absence from Argentina did little to improve the freedom of press in the field of journalism. Censorship was still practiced, magazines were still being shut down because of content, and journalists were still being imprisoned, among other reasons, for daring to use the name "Perón" in their columns.

The magazine *Primera Plana* was launched in 1962 as an Argentine version of *Time* or *Newsweek*. It was attractive and distinctive although expensive (the cost was equal to that of six newspapers). The magazine, produced principally by a younger generation, was filled with novelties, among them the need imposed on all journalists to check all details in their stories with at least two sources. The magazine included a variety of topics and acquired a great deal of influence throughout the country (Ulanovsky 1997, 150).

Panorama ("The magazine of our time") was another magazine with great circulation in the 1960s, among other reasons for the audacious reporting of a young reporter, Adriana Civitas (Ulanovsky 1997, 154). Civitas was a relentless reporter who went undercover to infiltrate organizations and gain first-hand information. *Panorama* was accused of being a magazine given to exploiting emotions; some called it "sensationalist" (Ulanovsky 1997, 155). No one at the magazine was offended and circulation soared.

On page 22 of issue 99 of *Primera Plana* Argentines caught their first glimpse of a little girl who would become popular throughout the world, Mafalda. Mafalda was the cartoon creation of Joaquín Lavado ("Quino"). This precocious eight-year-old child became the voice of many in the country who were concerned about Argentina's political and social problems. To use a little girl was a way for Quino to show that the problems of the country were so large that even a child could see them.

Mafalda conveyed simple truths about Argentine reality. What is interesting to note is that, because of the apparent innocence of the strip and its massive circulation, it was as powerful, or perhaps even more so, than many of the guerilla movements of the 1960s and 1970s. The diffusion of Mafalda throughout the world can be said to be parallel with the writings of such Argentine literary icons as Jorge Luis Borges or Julio Cortázar (Foster 1989, 53).

Mafalda was able to see clearly the problems of the Argentine middle class. Her friends represented certain easily recognizable "types" of the middle class who chose to remain oblivious to the problems around them, often times preferring to remain blind to injustices in the name of a false patriotism. As David William Foster has noted, "A significant aspect of the strip is that the other characters rarely understand fully the meaning of what Mafalda says" (Foster 1989, 54).

Both right and left denounced Quino: the government for his criticisms that were perceived to be somewhat "smart-aleck"; and the leftist organizations because they felt he was too tame (Foster 1989, 54). In 1973 Quino, tired of the criticisms that were leveled at him, decided to stop drawing his cartoon altogether, succumbing to the sociocultural repression of the day.

On December 23, 1965, the magazine *Confirmado* published a future chronology of what its editors believed was going to happen in Argentina over the next year. One of the predictions was that, within the next six months, a coup d'état, or overthrow of the government, would occur. As it turned out, the magazine was off by only three days. On June 28, 1966, the government of Arturio Illia fell and was replaced by another. The man behind the startling prediction was Jacobo Timerman, one of the most important journalists of the day. He based his information on logic and history. The military had never accepted Illia as president, and Timerman assumed that they would try to remove him from office before the annual military celebrations, scheduled for July 9, took place. General Juan Carlos Onganía became president of Argentina and censored or closed down "for a lack of respect to the authorities" many magazines and newspapers. Onganía made it difficult for the newspapers to obtain the resources they needed to publish their papers, and he detained a number of journalists (Ulanovsky 1997, 175).

Jacobo Timerman was the creative force behind both *Primera Plana* and *Confirmado*, two magazines that were of great importance in the country during the 1960s. They reflected a generally liberal ideology and a desire to keep Argentines abreast of news about the avant-garde and the innovative in the areas of the arts and literature. Both magazines also published articles about the abuses of the military and the censorship of certain cultural manifestations. They continued to publish interviews with political leaders of those parties that had been banned in the country (1997, 179–81). These activities did not make Timerman very popular among the generals.

In 1969 president Juan Carlos Onganía ordered that the publication of the magazine *Primera Plana* be stopped immediately and permanently for revealing information about disputes that he had had with general Alejandro Lanusse. In 1970 the magazine was able to resume publication legally, but it never regained its previous popularity.

In the early 1970s Tomás Eloy Martínez began to publish a series of interviews that he had conducted with Juan Perón in Madrid in the magazine *Panorama.* In 1971 Perón bought the journal *Primera Plana* in an effort to control at least one source of information in Argentina while still residing in Spain, reverting back to the tactics that he had employed while president.

Timerman founded another newspaper, *La Opinión*, in 1971, one that many would consider the greatest of his career. It was an important evolutionary step in the history of Argentine papers because, for the first time, an effort was made to dedicate the paper to select topics discussed in depth. Timerman's belief was, "Ten news items in one day are useful and comprehensible, one hundred, one can handle, but one thousand are overwhelming and unnecessary" (Ulanovsky 1997, 208). The model for such an undertaking was the French newspaper *Le Monde.* The idea was that there would be certain themes that a reader would be able to follow throughout the various editions of the journal, and all articles would be signed by the journalists who wrote them, providing the reader with a particular style with which he or she could identify.

In the mid-1970s the country witnessed a series of rapid changes. First, general Alejandro Lanusse, the president of the country, stepped down in May 1973. Héctor José Cámpora had won in free elections. He held the presidency for all of forty-nine days before Raúl Lastiri took control until everything was arranged for the return of General Juan Perón.

At the time, guerrilla movements throughout the country were on the rise, and in 1973 the director of *Clarín*, Bernardo Sofovich, was kidnapped in exchange for ransom and the publication of three manifestos. The government reacted by accusing the newspaper of being an accomplice to subversion and sent thirty armed civilians to the building where Sofovich was scheduled to give a press conference. They threw incendiary bombs which wounded some of those present and did significant damage to the building.

In 1975 sixteen actors, writers, and journalists received threats from the Anticommunist Alliance of Argentina (AAA). The director of the newspaper *El Día* in La Plata, David Kraiselburd, was kidnapped on June 25, 1974. Twenty days later, by accident, the police found where he was being hidden. When the *montoneros* (guerrilla group) saw the police they immediately killed their hostage. On October 13, 1974, another journalist was killed, Pedro Leopoldo Barraza. On May 19, 1975, yet another journalist, Jorge Money of *La Opinión*, was murdered.

A climate of fear reigned. Censorship was implemented with a threat of a term of from two to six years in prison for anyone who dared disturb the "national peace" (Ulanovsky 1997, 240). Isabel Perón, on the death of her husband, closed numerous magazines and newspapers. Many journalists went into exile during 1974 and 1975 when the violence rose to new heights. Journalists were now one of the most persecuted groups in the country. Tomás Eloy Martínez, one of Argentina's greatest journalists, has lived in exile since 1974; he is currently a professor at Rutgers University.

La Opinión was hit especially hard by the repression. A campaign was launched to discredit its director, Jacobo Timerman; death threats were made against many of its journalists; and any company that financially supported the newspaper or placed ads in it was threatened. There was also a chilling new requirement that all journalists for the paper publish all of their sources. It was also thought that the military leaders were behind the deaths of two of *La Opinión*'s most noted journalists, Pedro Barraza and Jorge Money.

On March 24, 1976, another coup d'état occurred. The generals launched what would be called the Process of National Reorganization, or *Proceso*. The generals promised to wipe out guerrilla activity and restore public order. The directors of all magazines and newspapers were informed of exactly what would be expected of them under the new order. It would be necessary for each journalist to have every article reviewed by a military official who would grant authority for it to be published. Anyone who did not subject his or her article to review would be sentenced to prison for as many as ten years. All newspapers were henceforth required to publish basically the same news. Since it was impossible, logistically, to do this, official censorship was replaced by self-censorship.

It must be clarified here that, at the beginning, the arrival of the generals was generally greeted by the population with relief. It was clear to everyone that something had to be done, and this was seen as a solution, even by those who were generally against the military. What awaited the country, however, was almost beyond imagination. Rafael Perrota, the director of *El Cronista* was kidnapped and tortured in a detention center. His body was never found, although Jacobo Timerman recognized him in one of the camps where he, too, was held (Ulanovsky 1997, 252).

Rodolfo Walsh was the first journalist to defy the military leaders openly. He wrote his "Open Letter from a Writer to the Military Junta" in 1977, printed it, and distributed it himself. He was in hiding at the time but when he was found, he was kidnapped, tortured, and killed. Many other journalists "disappeared" at the hands of the military, most notably Jacobo Timerman, the director of *La Opinión*, who was taken in April 1977. He remained imprisoned for thirty months and during that time learned first-hand the anti-Semitic strand of the *Proceso*. He was tortured and his citizenship was revoked. His life was finally saved, though it is unclear who saved him, and he was expelled from the country.

It was during this time that the magazine *Humor* appeared. For many it was a blessing. It was dangerous to launch a humor magazine in a country ruled by military authorities not known for a sense of humor, but it was thought that the Argentine people desperately needed to laugh in the midst of the violence and fear that gripped the country. As Juan Sasturain noted, it was like "continuing to dance as the *Titanic* was sinking" (quoted in Ulanovsky 1997, 277). Although the magazine was launched as one dedicated to humor, it was clear that one could read between the lines, and understand what was being conveyed.

On April 30 the Mothers of the Plaza de Mayo held their first meeting. Soon, journalists began to accompany them as they circled the plaza, including international journalists such as Gerard Albouy from *Le Monde*. Robert Cox of the *Buenos Aires Herald* also reported on the Mothers and maintained a section of the paper dedicated to publishing information about the disappearances of family members. When death threats against him began to include threats against his eleven-year-old son, he decided it was time to leave the city.

When the War of the Malvinas, or Falklands War, began in 1982, the military imposed rules on all the media: radio, television, newspapers, and magazines. The media could in no way question official information provided by the military; they could not admit that Argentina was not winning the war, even when it became clear that the country had already been defeated. When Argentine troops surrendered, the press was forbidden to use the word "surrender" and had to use euphemisms. Anyone who did not follow the rules could be immediately detained. Certain photos were falsified and printed in the press, including one of five Argentine soldiers stepping on "Malvinas" land with the Argentine flag.

It was an Italian journalist, Oriana Fallaci, who finally confronted one of the military presidents, Leopoldo Galtieri, in June 1982 and asked, "Isn't it possible that those little islands represented in your eyes an easy way to unite a country that was divided and unhappy, to try to make it forget about the inflation, about the the monstruous external debt or about the political and economic failure of the military regime that you represent?" (Ulanovsky 1997, 301). She was not detained, but the general made certain that she understood that anyone in Argentina who had dared to ask such a question would have been dealt with immediately in the harshest possible manner.

Essentially, the failure of the Malvinas War meant that it was just a matter of time before the end of the military government. The Mothers of the Plaza de Mayo had now become known throughout the world. Magazines and newspapers began to openly criticize the leaders. In 1983, number 97 of the magazine *Humor* was banned in the country because it openly poked fun at the generals.

During the years immediately before the *Proceso* and the *Proceso* itself, the amount of readers was a mere 50 percent of what it had been prior to those years. The press suffered a credibility problem with the public after the Malvinas War. Just prior to 1973, the five principal papers in the country sold as many as 2 million copies per day. In 1983, eleven papers in Buenos Aires were unable to sell more than 1,100,000. Clearly, this pointed to a growing unease in the public with the press and the media in general.

In 1987 journalist Rodolfo Bracelli published an article in *Plural* about the top subjects that were discussed in the press during the years of the dictatorship, other than the World Cup of 1978. Not surprisingly, the most reported story during those years of bloodshed and fierce repression was that of the marriage of Susana Giménez and Carlos Monzón, two popular television personalities. The *Proceso* had meant closures, disappearances of journalists, destruction of facilities, firings, threats, bomb threats, official censorship, self-censorship, and exile. More than 100 journalists were imprisoned and tortured, and twice that number were living in exile. It was clear that the press was one of the casualties of the dictatorship.

In 1983 Raúl Alfonsín became the president of Argentina. Although technically the press was now free to operate, the economic situation of the country declined dramatically. Because there was little paper, it was necessary to reduce the number of the pages. There was less investment by companies for publicity, greater unemployment among workers connected to the media, strikes of employees, and decline in circulation. In 1984 Timerman returned to Argentina from exile to take control of *La Razón*. It was not a success.

In 1987 the final paper that would become important, *Página/12*, was launched. The director of the paper selected people to serve on his staff from the Opera café on the corner of Corrientes and Callao streets. He wrote a summary of his articles on their napkins. It was an odd beginning for a paper that would become one of the most influential in the country (Ulanovsky 1997, 332). One of the early writers for the paper said later, "We didn't have paper, chairs, desks or typewriters but we had more than enough passion" (332). The idea behind the paper, according to its founders, Jorge Lanata and Ernesto Tiffenberg, was that there were very few things that needed to be reported about on a daily basis. The paper dealt with topics that previously had been rarely mentioned, such as minority groups, gays, lesbians, feminists, human rights activists, and so on. The newspaper would deal with only five or six main stories each day. It would print debates, articles, and editorials that did not necessarily reflect the opinion of its director.

Página/12 sought to push the limits of what could be said. It has remained true to that ideal to this day. It was a progressive paper, which was troubling to its competitors. As a consequence, although it has suffered numerous threats and has been seen as a threat to both Alfonsín and Menem, it continues to do well. It came into being in a tumultous time in Argentine history, the 1980s, during which the country saw six presidents, four military leaders, and two civilian leaders. The country began the decade in a dictatorship and ended with one elected president passing the presidential stick to another, the first time since 1928 that a transfer of power had occurred between two civilian leaders.

In the 1990s many of Argentina's magazines and newspapers may be found on the World Wide Web. The first to use the World Wide Web was *El Cronista* in 1994. Now others, such as *Clarín, La Nación, Ámbito Financiero, Los Andes* from Mendoza and *Hoy* from La Plata, are also online. Their Websites often contain databanks for researching earlier editions. Argentine news, for the first time, is now available to more than 30 million people on five continents.

BROADCAST MEDIA

Argentine radio, born on August 27, 1920, was begun by a group of young pioneers known as the "crazy guys of the neighborhood." Neither engineers nor inventors, they were all young people in their early twenties from Barrio Norte, a wealthy neighborhood in Buenos Aires. One of the young men was already a doctor, and the others were studying medicine. They loved music and theater and had active imaginations. They followed with a passion the news about the great Italian inventor Guglielmo Marconi who had patented the first radiotelegraph in England in 1896. When Marconi arrived in Argentina in 1910, he was able to communicate with bases in Canada and Ireland, which fueled the burning interest in the "crazy ones" to bring the novelty permanently to Argentina.

News to Argentina slowed during World War I. Nevertheless, the young Argentines followed with great attention the news that, in the United States, David Sarnoff was able to transmit news and music via the radio for the first time in 1916. In 1917 the president of Argentina, Hipólito Yrigoyen, made the first formal decree controlling radio. It was thought that any radio buff in the country would be able to use the radio to tell the Germans about the movements of the boats in the port; as a result, radio transmission was prohibited. It was not until the peace treaty was signed in 1918 that the use of radio for artistic purposes was allowed.

The first radio transmission for the benefit of the general public occurred on August 27, 1920; a concert of Richard Wagner's *Parsifal* was broadcast from the Coliseo theater in Buenos Aires. Only sixty-seven days after *Parsifal* was transmitted by the new Society of Argentine Radio, a station in Pittsburgh, Pennsylvania, KDKA, went on the air with the first interview of a presidential candidate, Warren G. Harding.

In the 1920s and 1930s radio went through some rapid changes in Argentina. Transmissions were sent not only from the Coliseo but also from the Colón and the new Cervantes theater. There were many "firsts" in those years, among them, in 1922, the first Argentine president to be heard on the

The Teatro Colón, the largest opera house in South America. Courtesy of Eduardo Gil.

radio, Marcelo Torcuato de Alvear. A number of radio stations emerged to join Radio Argentina, including Radio Cultura, Radio Sudamérica, and Radio Brusa (Ulanovsky 1997, 33). Radio Cultura was the first to arrange payment for publicity announced on their shows. Radio Brusa was the first to have programming of popular and dance music. These new stations did not play continuously but rather on certain days and at certain times. In the mid-1920s the first radio contests were presented, and sometimes the products that a company was trying to sell on the air would be the only payment received by the radio artists. In the early days, radio was used in many ways. At one point an exercise program was broadcast that required the radio listeners to look at the illustrations of the exercises published in the magazine *Radiolandia* and, accompanied by lively piano music, to practice them at home.

In the 1930s radio theater began with the program *Chispazos de tradición*. The program was the brainchild of an immigrant from Spain, José Andrés Gonzales Pulido, who wanted to present to Argentines a program devoted to the legends of the gauchos. He hit upon one of the key components necessary to develop a devoted audience: the cliffhanger. Women would often wait outside the studio to hit the "villain" from the series when he emerged from the station, a tribute to the great emotion generated by the show. *Chispazos* changed the daily lives of Argentines; even the phone company reported that during the times the program was transmitted, fewer calls were placed throughout the city.

In 1930 the inhabitants of Buenos Aires were able to hear the World Cup from speakers that were set up on the Avenida de Mayo. The listeners gathered on the sidewalk in front of the station, and the crowd got so big that it spilled over into the street and blocked traffic. The connection of sports to radio was established and continued to grow over the years. Other radio innovations of the 1930s include the program *Ronda Policial* in which crime in the city was reported and occasionally reenacted with sound effects.

In 1935 Radio El Mundo opened its state-of-the-art studios on Maipú Street at 555. The building, referred to as "the Temple," inspired awe in all that came to see it. The first edifice ever designed specifically for radio in Argentina, it had seven studios, the largest of which was able to accommodate 500 spectators. Radio El Mundo had its own orchestra and put on shows from morning to evening. With the inauguration of Radio El Mundo, radio in Argentina entered into its golden age.

Radio also played a pivotal role in the lives of Argentina's most internationally well-known figures, beloved tango singer Carlos Gardel and the former first lady, Eva Perón. Gardel was first heard on the radio in 1924 and it was through the diffusion of his music through radio and movies, as well as records, that Gardel became famous throughout the world. In November 1933 Gardel performed for the last time on Argentine radio, singing the tango "Buenos Aires." When he died in a plane crash in 1935, all the country mourned the loss. For one entire week no radio station played any tango music to express the country's grief.

Eva Perón, probably the most well-known woman in Argentine history, had an intimate connection with radio throughout her short life as well. She first arrived at the studios of Radio Belgrano in 1937. She worked there for many years, although at that time radio personalities were rarely paid. The people that helped her through that hungry, difficult time in her life were repaid on a grand scale when she became the first lady of Argentina in 1946.

It was in late January 1944, at a benefit held on behalf of the victims of an earthquake in San Juan, Argentina, that Eva is said to have first met General Juan Domingo Perón. He appeared at the studios of Radio Belgrano in early February to attend radio shows in which she participated. His presence in the studio was covered by all of the magazines of the day including *Antena* and *Radiolandia*. At the time, it was common for radio personalities to appear on the cover of these magazines and for stories about them to abound inside the pages, alongside the programming information. In June of that same year Eva was seen with Perón for the first time at a public function held at the Colón. The generals and society's elite were scandalized that he would be seen on the arm of a young radio starlet.

When Eva died on July 26, 1952, the entire country came to a halt to listen to a solemn voice intoning, "The Subsecretary of Information is fulfilling his very sad duty of informing the people of the Republic that at 20: 25 Eva Perón, spiritual leader of the country, died." The country went into a period of mourning that lasted for sixteen days. Radios played only solemn music, occasionally interrupted by someone reading sections of Eva's autobiography, *La razón de mi vida* (The reason for my life). Although the radios resumed regular programming after the official mourning period had ended, each evening, for as long as Perón was in power, at exactly 20:25 (8:25), the following announcement was made: "It is 20:25, the hour that Eva Perón entered into immortality."

Radio itself suffered a great deal of censorship during the years of Perón's reign. His solution to receiving bad press was simply to buy out the stations and newspapers and force them to publish articles and stories that were favorable to him. In 1943 a law was passed by the generals that 90 percent of all programming on radios had to be Argentine and only 10 percent could be international. Another decree stated that only the most grammatically correct form of Spanish could be spoken on the airwaves. The generals felt it was in the best interest of the country to "clean up" the language and felt that by imposing such laws people would be forced to comply. Of course, that meant banning some of the most popular radio personalities of the day, including Niní Marshall, who had a whole repertoire of characters that came from the spectrum of Argentine "types," often immigrants; most of these would not be recognizable to the listening public if speaking in the Spanish from Spain were required. The generals, however, felt that Niní set a poor example for the country. The star went to Uruguay and continued to work on radio there, and Argentines simply listened to her on Radio Colonia, a habit that would resume in all periods of repression during the years that followed.

In 1940 one of the most popular programs in Argentina's radio history began to be heard, *Los Pérez García*. The radio program was meant to present Argentines with a family with which they would be able to identify. They did, and in massive numbers. Argentines thought that the Pérez García characters were just like them, just like their neighbors, and that they understood their needs and interests. They were like friends who entered the living rooms of Argentine households. Their intrigues, loves, and losses became those of all who listened. The show continued to be an important presence in Buenos Aires until it finally ended in 1966.

By 1944, 1.2 million radios were in use in the country. Quiz shows were all the rage, and another radio soap opera became popular: *¡Qué pareja!* stayed on the airwaves until 1969 (Ulanovsky 1995, 164). *¡Qué pareja!*, *Los Pérez García*, and two other very popular shows, *Peter Fox lo sabía* and *Glostora Tango Club*, dominated the airwaves well into the 1950s and in some cases through the 1960s.

During the 1950s radio continued to be the most popular medium in the country. There was, at that time, a radio in virtually every house. Television was introduced in the country in 1951, but there was only one station, Channel 7, and it was owned by the government. Perón dominated the radio from 1946 to 1951, and from 1951 to 1955 he dominated the medium of television as well.

Enrique Susini, one of the original "locos," became one of the camera directors for the first transmission of television in Argentina, Radio Belgrano Televisión, on October 17, 1951. He was also a dedicated enthusiast of the new genre of of film. In fact, he was involved in radio, film, television, theater, and opera—all while continuing to practice medicine. He dedicated his entire life to embarking on projects deemed impossible by others.

In the 1950s the *Pérez García* show continued its popular run. In 1955 the actor who played the role of the father, Martín Zabalúa, died, and it was decided that another actor would not replace him. The role of the *Pérez García* mother would become a widow. When the radio started a contest to find out when two characters of the *Pérez García* program should marry, 305,884 people responded by sending in letters. The listening public set the date of September 21, 1955.

When Perón was deposed in 1955, the media that he had controlled to be solidly in his favor was required, by a new law, to move into the opposite extreme. All references to the former leader were now forbidden, although clever radio announcers knew how to talk about him without using his name. In 1957 Niní Marshall was allowed to return to the radio in Buenos Aires. The University of La Plata even asked her to make recordings of her most famous characters in order to have them preserved in their archives.

The domain of radio was never really threatened by the advent of television in Argentina until 1960. It is said that Eva Perón was the driving force behind the establishment of the country's first station in 1951. By the late 1940s she was enthralled with having yet another medium to spread the message of Perón to the people. She implored her former boss, Jaime Yankelevich of

A political demonstration in the Plaza de Mayo in front of the Casa Rosada. Such concentrations were made popular by Peronismo in the 1940s and 1950s. Courtesy of Eduardo Gil.

Radio Belgrano, to make a trip to the United States and buy equipment. He returned and the launching of television was scheduled to take place on Peronist Loyalty Day, October 17, 1960. The first image transmitted to television viewers on that day was that of a smiling Eva, and the first "show" was the massive rally being staged in front of the Plaza de Mayo in honor of Perón (Morgan and Shanahan 1995, 35; Sirvén 1988, 22).

The state controlled one television channel throughout the decade of the 1960s. In 1960, however, two private television stations were added. The following year yet another was launched, bringing the total to four. Televisions also were within reach of middle-class Argentines for the first time. As a result, a profound crisis gripped the radio business throughout the decade.

Many of the orchestras that had been part of the radio stations disbanded or went to television. Many of the programs that had been so famous on radio were transformed into similar programs on television. The *Pérez García* niche was filled by *La familia Falcón*, and the quiz shows went to television as well. It was as though all of the best that radio had to offer in the past was now taken by television and what remained for radio was music and news.

On the positive side, the technology in records had improved immensely, and the stigma that for so long had been attached to the use of records for radio programming diminished. Cassette tapes were also introduced to the public and became an important part of radio programming. Another positive development in the 1960s was that radio announcers began to improvise, abandoning their strict adherence to the written script and allowing themselves to be spontaneous. The dividing line was established between radio personalities who could merely read and those who were capable of thinking on their feet—the medium would never be the same.

Many of the popular radio figures moved to television, but some were able to perform on both media. "Pinky," Lidia Elsa Satragno, was a success in both media with her programs. The 1966 World Cup played in England would be the last World Cup that the majority of Argentines would experience via radio. The next one, from Mexico, was broadcast live on television.

The 1960s were said to be the golden age of television in Argentina. The three major networks in the United States, ABC, NBC, and CBS, had strong ties to the three private television channels in Buenos Aires. Argentines were exposed to many of the programs in the United States and emulated those of the poorest quality, sometimes for the better, as a few of the soap operas survived into the 1990s, but generally for the worse.

In 1967 a strange law was passed by the secretary of communications for Radio Nacional. Seventy percent of all of its airtime had to be music, the rest oral. Forty percent of the 70 percent had to be classical music, 34 percent light music, 15 percent native music, and 11 percent popular music. This sort of precision would be echoed in later governmental decrees throughout the 1970s, leaving radio directors in a constant state of panic, trying to make the calculations every day in order to avoid arrest.

In 1972, in a suspicious fire, the beautiful building of Radio El Mundo at Maipú 555, the Temple, was destroyed. At the time it housed five stations. Throughout the 1970s, as violence became widespread, more and more people began to listen to Uruguayan radio. When Perón died in 1974, the government required Radio Colina, in Uruguay, to play music that would dignify the period of mourning; the station was unable to comply because they had no such music at the station. The military was in charge in 1973 in Uruguay so it became difficult for Argentines to get information via their neighbor's transmissions. In fact, when Radio Colonia announced information in 1975 about the death of Spanish dictator Francisco Franco, explaining exactly who he had been to their listeners, the Uruguayan military government closed the station down for having shown "disrespect."

In September 1974, the government passed another decree regarding radio broadcasting. This time all stations were required to play 75 percent national music—25 percent music by Argentine composers or singers, 25 percent folkloric music, and 25 percent music from Buenos Aires (tangos, milongas). In 1976, when the coup d'état took place, the state radio systems were practically paralyzed. During this time of uncertainty and violence, the radio producers and announcers suffered from censorship, program suspensions, and station closures. In October 1976 a list of certain national and international musicians unacceptable to the regime was given to the radio stations. The list included the Beatles, Brazil's Chico Buarque de Hollanda, and, much to everyone's surprise, Carlos Gardel.

Clearly it was felt that the prohibition of the country's most beloved musician had to be a mistake. The authorities were approached to find out what sort of ideological or aesthetic justification could be behind such an absurd proclamation. It was discovered that the law had been put into effect because a navy captain's wife did not like Gardel (Ulanovsky 1995, 333). It was difficult to work under such odd conditions of censorship, and radio lapsed into what many have referred to as a bland sort of mediocre programming.

Television did not fare much better. The only topic certain not to incite the wrath of the generals was soccer, so those years saw extended sports coverage. Other than soccer, television primarily offered tourist information concerning Argentine travel destinations and comedy shows (Sirvén 1988, 37). The television stars and writers suffered the same fate as many of their media colleagues and many opted for exile amid the mounting violence.

In 1979 something new was introduced. FM radio had arrived, and, although it was considered to be the domain of the young, FM was able to develop top-rate programming. As Carlos Ulanovsky points out, the FM radio programs showed "audacity, a bit of craziness, creativity, and rebellion, as well as iconoclasm, a fresh quality and a direct and informal language much like that one would hear in the street" (1995, 346).

In the early 1980s television and radio were standard fare for everyone in the country. Lunch was eaten with one of the most important figures in Argentine television, Mirtha Legrand, who hosted her talk show with an enormous portrait of herself hanging directly behind her. In 1980 sixteen women were called to the offices of General Albano Harguindeguy. These were women, according to the general, who transmitted information and formed opinions, and they needed to understand their important role in society. At one point he mentioned self-censorship of those in the press. It was then that he was interrupted by one of the journalists, Magdalena Ruiz Guiñazú, who insisted that he knew perfectly well that the censorship was not merely self-imposed but rather imposed by the military. "You would know better than I do," the courageous reporter said. The general replied that he would be happy to have knowledge of even 30 percent of what was happening under the military government.

When the Malvinas war broke out, there were 635 Argentine deaths and the country, one would think, would be forced to acknowledge defeat. During the war, the media had helped create an artificial state of euphoria among listeners and viewers because the media were forced to report only hyperbolic accounts of battles that portrayed Argentines as the valiant victors. No opinion unfavorable to the military was allowed and, as a result, when the truth was revealed, many people lost all confidence in the media. The television viewing public declined dramatically at that time.

After the demise of the dictatorship, radio and television producers were able to speak openly again but they found that the recent episode of brutal dictatorship in many cases was simply too painful to discuss or for that matter to listen to (Ulanovsky 1995, 364). Many of the radio and television stations that began to discuss these themes suffered threats. In 1985 one group detonated powerful explosives at Radio Belgrano. The feeling was that one did not want to irritate the military and provide them with any excuse to return to power. Nonetheless, radio and television were present and covered the most important demonstrations of the day in defense of democracy, including one in 1987 in which 400,000 people participated.

Oddly enough, as in the press and the theater, the postdictatorship period was among the least creative in terms of the quality of output in television (Sirvén 1988, 53). Although it may have been due to the large numbers of previously censored international shows and films that were now allowed to be broadcast, it is troubling nonetheless.

One of the oddest and most pervasive characteristics of Argentine television noted by critics has been the rise and expansion of programs dedicated to giving prizes to viewers who call or write in. The most popular example of this remains the program ¡Hola Susana! with Susana Giménez. The prize-giving gimmick has been seen by many to be the result of a lack of quality in programming. Viewers are essentially enticed and bought by greed, boredom, or desperation to participate (Sirvén 1988, 225). One of the most unusual examples of this occurred in 1994 when an entire hour was dedicated to calls from viewers who were trying to guess the correct weight of a slice of apple in order to win a prize.

Another example that actually borders on the grotesque was the strange idea introduced in 1994 to have adolescents write in to a Buenos Aires news program in an effort to win money for their grandparents by answering one question correctly about Argentine history or current events. The reasoning behind this had to do with the crisis that hit the elderly in the late 1980s and early 1990s. The government simply was unable to provide them with the finances they needed for retirement, in spite of the fact that these individuals had been promised a sort of "social security" during their entire lives. The situation has been characterized as one of the saddest of these recent years of Argentine "democracy." The elderly are given barely enough each month to survive, and they protest their plight each week in front of the national congress. In any event, the spectacle of watching a child, knowing that the fate of grandma or grandpa, is in his or her hands, was disconcerting. Even worse, the grandparent appeared on camera with the child and could be seen in a close-up as the child, sometimes stammering, sweating profusely, or suffering any number of nervous tics, tried to answer the question. For those who answered correctly, there were smiles and hugs all around. Those who failed will undoubtedly recount that excruciating moment in therapy for many years to come.

In 1989 a totally unique program was introduced to the radio audience, Mario Pergolini's *Malas compañías* (Bad company). The objective was to provide a forum for Argentines to speak openly about all of the unspeakable topics of the day, not only those related to the dictatorship but also other issues, such as homosexuality, drug addiction, and other topics. A tremendous hit, it was a new stage in the development of radio that brought it into the 1990s.

By 1995 there were an average of 5.4 radios per household, and 63 percent of the population of Buenos Aires said that the radio was their first source of information. By the mid-1990s cable television had become common throughout the country and with cable came transmissions from around the world with over sixty channels to choose from the best to the worst of international programming. This selection was added to the game shows, dance parties, and soap operas that remain common fare on the national stations. Computers with immediate access not only to world press but also to international radio and television have also begun to become common among the wealthier Argentines and are rapidly becoming more affordable for all. The effect of the virtual overload of information remains to be seen and studied but the prospects are exciting.

REFERENCES

Bernhardson, Wayne. *Argentina, Uruguay and Paraguay: A Lonely Planet Travel Survival Kit.* Hawthorn, Australia: Lonely Planet, 1996.

Foster, David William. *From Mafalda to the Supermachos: Latin American Graphic Humor as Popular Culture.* Boulder, Colo.: Lynne Rienner Publishers, 1989.

Fraser, Howard. *Magazines and Masks: Caras y caretas as a Reflection of Buenos Aires, 1898–1908.* Tempe: Center for Latin American Studies, Arizona State University, 1987.

Morgan, Michael, and James Shanahan. *Democracy Tango: Television, Adolescents, and Authoritarian Tensions in Argentina.* Cresskill, N.J.: Hampton Press, 1995.

Sirvén, Pablo. *Quien te ha visto y quien T.V.* Buenos Aires: Ediciones de la Flor, 1988.

Ulanovsky, Carlos. *Días de radio: historia de la radio argentina.* 5th ed. Buenos Aires: Espasa Cape, 1995.

———. *Paren las rotativas: historia de los grandes diarios, revistas y periodista argentinos.* Buenos Aires: Espasa Cape, 1997.

Walsh, Rodolfo. *El oficio violento de escribir.* Buenos Aires: Planeta, 1995.

5

Cinema

ARGENTINA is one of the leading filmmaking countries of Latin America, a position it shares with Mexico, Brazil, and, to a lesser extent, Cuba. However, there are significant differences among these countries. Cuba has had an extensive production in the context of the Castro revolution and regime, which came to power in 1959. Despite the severe economic conditions that Cuba is presently experiencing, first-rate filmmaking has continued with support from Radio-Televisión Española. Mexico, unlike virtually all other Latin American republics, has had continuous institutional stability since the period following the 1910 revolution. Consequently, Mexico has an extensive filmmaking infrastructure including considerable government support that serves not only the large national audience, but also exports Mexican films (today mostly in the form of cassettes) to Spanish-speaking communities in the United States and to other Latin American republics, especially in the Caribbean and Central America. Mexican art films have enjoyed an enormous American and international audience, which includes most of the Latin American republics. Brazil, while counting on large internal markets like Argentina and Mexico and enjoying periods of important government support, has had periods of censorship that have seriously reduced or circumscribed national production. More important, because Brazilians speak Portuguese rather than Spanish, only subtitled versions can be shown in the rest of Latin America and the world. Latin Americans may be willing to view Hollywood films with subtitles or, in the case of more sophisticated audiences, German, British, French, or Japanese films with subtitles, but the distribution of Brazilian films with subtitles, with the exception of a few blockbusters, has always been problematical. This is due in part to a historical isolation of Brazil vis-à-vis the rest of Latin America and especially Argentina. However, recent programs of regional economic integration are resulting in greater cultural exchange, which surely will affect film distribution.

Argentina, like Mexico, has made major contributions to the Latin American film industry and historically has had good mechanisms for internal and external distribution and has been able to count on various forms of government support. However, authoritarian and tyrannical governments have placed a heavy hand on filmmaking. Such governments have mandated certain production formulas, as during the Peronista period, from 1946 to 1955. Or they have imposed far-reaching forms of censorship (including the banning and cutting of foreign films, which have traditionally been so important in establishing a national film culture), particularly during the neofascist governments that ruled in the years 1966–1973 and 1976–1983. Current neoliberal economic policies, which have been important in maintaining stability during the new democratic period that opened in 1983, have meant what often seems like a wholesale replacement of national culture by foreign imports. The policies have also meant the disappearance of the neighborhood theater, along with a considerable reduction of downtown and mainline art houses, and their replacement by video stores that are reluctant to carry national films because of the high demand for Hollywood films. At the present time, national films are showcased in only one movie house. In other commercial houses they frequently experience short and unprofitable runs. On a more positive note, national films, including the great titles of the national repertoire, may now be seen on television (including special cable access), often accompanied by the sort of erudite and urbane commentary that has long characterized film culture in Argentina. One might note here that film reviewing for major Buenos Aires newspapers continues to be highly regarded professionally and intellectually.

Primitive forms of film arrived in Argentina at approximately the same time as in other parts of the West. The first public exhibition of film took place on July 18, 1896, in the Teatro Odeón, a variety-show house that still exists in downtown Buenos Aires. The showing consisted of several of Auguste and Louis Lumière's shorts, including the famous "Arrival of a Train," which gave the audience the sensation of a train speeding toward them. This clip, widely used in promotional material for filmmaking, served effectively to engage the spectator with the new cluster of sensations that film was to depend on for its commercial success.

The decade beginning in 1910 in Argentina was a period of intense beginnings, enhanced by World War I. As in the case of World War II, the interruption in the availability of films from Europe and the United States (during World War II, this was a result of Argentina's alleged neutral, but actually pro-Axis, stance) stimulated local production. In 1915 Eduardo Martínez de la Pera and Enrique Gunche released *Nobleza gaucha* (Gaucho nobility), based on motifs related to the cowboys of the Pampas and one of Argentina's abiding cultural icons. This film was remade as a talkie in 1937 by Sebastián M. Naón. When sound came to the Argentine film in the 1930s, there began an intense participation of people drawn from the performing arts, notably from the radio and the variety hall. Carlos Gardel, another of Argentina's cultural icons owing to his successful commercialization of the tango as a song rather than just a dance, made numerous films in Argentina and in the United States before his death in an airplane accident in Colombia in 1935.

TORRE NILSSON

It is difficult to generalize about Argentine filmmaking, since it has been as varied as that of the United States, with the exception of the obvious limitation of resources that has, in recent years, prevented it from imitating the Hollywood blockbuster. Nevertheless, during the golden age of the 1930s–1950s, Argentina made sophisticated drawing-room comedies; versions of national myths, both urban and rural (gaucho movies were the equivalent of Hollywood oaters); hard-hitting social commentaries; goof-ball throwaways; interpretations of "universal" motifs (e.g., Romeo and Julieta, classical themes); films noirs; and highly intellectual art films. In the 1940s and 1950s, Leopoldo Torre Nilsson emerged as Argentina's first true film auteur. Basing many of his films on literary works, Torre Nilsson introduced highly experimental camera and structuring techniques that gave his films an intensely artistic polish. Despite his international interests, Torre Nilsson's work is profoundly Latin American and Argentine. Moreover, he has filmed several novels written by his wife, Beatriz Guido, who has also prepared other film scripts for him, giving his filmmaking a potentially feminist flavor that has yet to be explored.

One of Torre Nilsson's most viewed films internationally is *La casa del ángel* (The house of the angel, 1957), in which Guido's hand in the script is especially evident. The title of the film refers to an aristocratic mansion famous for the power brokers who, during the heyday of ward politics in Buenos Aires, met there to cut deals, to anoint candidates, to destroy the opposition, to distribute rewards for cooperating with the system, and to mete out punishments for not playing along. As a draconian symbol of the vast realm and unquestioned power of the patriarchy, the house becomes a psychological space of terror for the young daughter of the family that lives there. Repressed on the one hand by the religious fanaticism of her mother and exposed to the raw masculinity of her father's henchmen, the girl is a study of dread and predestination in which the influence of Ingmar Bergman is as evident as is Torres Nilsson's desire to make a political statement about the destruction of the individual by a system whose coherency is the consequence of its efficient use of stragems to control others that have nothing to do with law or morality. The rape of the protagonist must be regarded not just as the victimization of women who are excluded from the political process while their bodies are brutally used by it. Rather, Torre Nilsson's feminine protagonists are as much figures of women's history as they are of all that which is excluded from masculine history, which includes men who do not adequately fulfill the masculinist imperatives of the patriarchy and are, as a consequence, as much "raped" by it as are women of conventional femininity. However, where *La casa del ángel* becomes an especially subtle film is in the representation of the patriarchy not just as a bloody political system, but as a dynamic whose brutality dooms it to its own destruction. It has been customary for critics to see Torre Nilsson's film—coming as it does soon after the Peronista's dramatic confrontations with the traditional power structure, which reasserted its control after Perón's fall in 1955—as an elaborate allegory of the Argentine oligarchy.

During periods of the relaxation of censorship at the end of periods of military dictatorships or during parentheses of democratic reinstitutionalization, notable films have been made dealing with tyranny and authoritarianism. The by now fairly secure period of democracy that has lasted since 1983 has seen the production of some truly notable works, including Argentina's first Oscar, the only one to have been won by a Latin American film.

THE OFFICIAL STORY

La historia oficial (The official story), which won the Oscar for the best foreign film of the year in 1986, was released in early March 1985 and had the advantage of making an immediate impact early in the year and a long lead time for foreign distribution before Oscar voting took place the following year. The film, directed by Luis Puenzo and based on a script written by Aída Bortnik, was part of the program of cultural redemocratization encouraged by the new constitutional government and, in many cases, underwritten by it. Stars like Héctor Alterio and Norma Aleandro, who had suffered persecution during the military regime (1976–1983), were joined by Bortnik, who had been involved in a protest theater movement at the end of the dictatorship, and María Elena Walsh, Argentina's premier composer of children's books and songs. Her theme song for the film is characteristic of her work—a simple, tuneful melody that bears a pointed subversive message.

The film centers on a business-class family (Alterio and Aleandro), who are about to celebrate the birthday of their daughter, whom they had adopted several years earlier. The time is the beginning of the school year in 1983, still nine months away from the departure of the military government, and Alicia (Aleandro) is seen in her professional life as a high school history teacher. Until she is reminded of events by an old school chum who returns to Argentina after years of exile following her imprisonment and torture by the military, Aleandro's character is not interested in looking too closely at recent Argentine history—at least, not too closely at the circumstances surrounding the sudden availability of an adoptive child in a country where, because of a very low birthrate, children for adoption are extremely rare. In European-oriented Buenos Aires, children of indigenous extraction (the so-called "black heads") are not desirable, and so the couple counts itself fortunate indeed to have a little girl who appears to come from their social class.

But Aleandro's character, who has suffered something like a tentative feminist awakening, begins to question her husband. Alterio's character has his own concerns because his business dealings, based on the deep corruption sustained during the military period, are beginning to fall apart because of the disgrace of the military in the Malvinas or Falklands War in 1982. The foregone conclusion is that the country will make a speedy transition to constitutional democracy. With that, has come the promise of investigations into corruption by the military and their civilian cohorts. Alterio is not amused by his wife's sudden interest in finding out where the child came from. Throughout the film, we see him engaging in increasingly violent reactions that end in open physical abuse, which can be interpreted as an extension of the repressive military rule.

Probably not many Argentine moviegoers in 1985, and certainly few foreign spectators, were prepared for what the mother eventually discovered— that her daughter had been taken from a young woman arrested for alleged terrorism. After giving birth to the child in prison, the woman was executed and her child given up for adoption. Not only were these children war booty for military officials and their civilian supporters, but their adoption was considered a Christian act. They were being saved from being raised by Godless subversives. Finding her formerly tranquil life verging on dissolution, with her husband almost out of his mind and her students almost openly

rebellious in their harsh criticism of the historical roots of Argentine authoritarianism, Alicia tries to find out about her daughter's biological family.
Her research leads her to a dead end at the hospital where her daughter was
born, but there she meets another woman who has run up against the silence
of the medical archives. This woman works with a group of Mothers of the
Disappeared, who have undertaken an intensive investigation into the
whereabouts of their disappeared children and other relatives (these "mad
women," as the military came to call them, have also become a veritable icon
of Argentine sociocultural history). In due course, the adoptive mother meets
an older woman who is in all likelihood the grandmother of the child in
question.

The film concludes with a dramatic confrontation between the two women
and Alterio's character and then between the parents. The film leaves unresolved the fate of the little girl. Will she remain with her adoptive parents
or, perhaps, with her mother, who leaves her husband, in the style of Ibsen's
Nora, after having been beaten by him? Perhaps she will remain with her
paternal grandparents, where she is while the dramatic confrontations are
taking place. Or should she be transferred to the care of her biological ma-
ternal grandmother? These quandaries, which had only begun to be addressed
at the time of the making of the film, are still unresolved in many cases
pending in Argentina a dozen years after the end of the military dictatorship.
The film is very effective in this regard. The final scene, as the credits roll,
shows the little girl rocking and singing Walsh's song, "The I-Don't-
Remember-Which Country." *La historia oficial* asked the audience not only
to face up to the horrors of the tyranny many of them had actively supported
as good therapy against the "excesses of democracy," but also to understand
how many issues had no solutions, which became clear during the actual
trials of military officials.[1]

Although *La historia oficial* is probably the most likely cultural product to
be named by students of Argentine culture relating to the postmilitary period,
the film has been criticized on at least two fronts. In the first place, it is a
very slick product. Although Argentine filmmaking has a long record of
imitating the features of the Hollywood package (sound quality has, however,
often been a problem), art films were likely to adhere to the principle of
"imperfect cinema" where, in order not to be slick, the filmic infrastructure
and its scarce resources were often in evidence. However, Puenzo, whose
roots are in the glossy advertising sector that is culturally very powerful in
Argentina, made a film that set a new standard for Argentine filmmaking: a
sociopolitically committed text that nevertheless made use of a commercial
film language and the best technical processes (including impeccable sound).

The second criticism leveled at *La historia oficial* is more strictly ideological in nature. By presenting an interpretation of recent Argentine history that focused on the actual agents of military rule, attributing all abuses to them, the film can be said to skim over the fact that the sort of authoritarianism represented by the dictatorship in its harshest and most naked forms is not confined to a period of repressive tyranny. It is a specific embodiment of the authoritarianism that is integral to Argentine daily life, and it has a long history in Argentine society, something which the history professor in the film appears to have trouble grasping. Official history becomes not just the imposed version of the military, but the way in which Argentine society as a whole wishes to avoid confronting its authoritarian bases. Concomitantly, the film engages in official historification by appearing to subscribe to the belief that the military high command and its supporters deserve all the blame for what happened. Furthermore, this version of an official history fails to underscore adequately how large sectors of the populace, not just self-serving fellow travelers, supported the military coup of 1976. Of course, no valid survey of public support was ever conducted. Nevertheless, it is important to understand how neofascist governments can legitimize themselves only if they have widespread support from the general population, no matter how quickly that support may subsequently vanish.

MARÍA LUISA BEMBERG

One film that has addressed the historical roots of authoritarianism is a good candidate for the second most famous film produced in Argentine under the sponsorship of redemocratization, María Luisa Bemberg's *Camila* (1984). Bemberg, who died in 1994, only became a filmmaker in her fifties; therefore, her work is confined basically to a ten-year period. Yet she has emerged as the most important feminist director in film history in Argentina as well as in Latin America. Her last film, *De eso no se habla* (I don't talk about it, 1993) starred Marcelo Mastroiani. It is a testimonial to the importance of Argentine filmmaking that several famous European stars have made films in Argentina in recent years: in 1993, Vanessa Redgrave starred in *Un muro de silencio* (A wall of silence), which was directed by Lita Stantic, the producer of Bemberg's *Camila*.

In 1848, Camila O'Gorman, pregnant, twenty-years old, and the daughter of one of dictator Juan Manuel Rosas's staunchest supporters, is executed along with her lover, a priest, Ladislao Gutiérrez. Camila had seduced Ladislao and convinced him that the two should flee from Buenos Aires in order to pursue their love as far as possible from the powerful reach of Rosas's dictatorship, but there were too many factors in play for them ever to hide successfully from Rosas. When they were finally discovered, captured, brought back to Buenos Aires, and executed together (in violation of the law and Catholic custom, which forbids the execution of a pregnant woman because it means necessarily also killing the unborn child), O'Gorman passed into Argentine legend as a symbol of the terrifying oppression of the forces of barbarism. Today the Argentine theme of "barbarism" (see the discussion on Domingo Faustino Sarmiento's influential *Civilización i barbarie* in Chapters 1 and 6) can be recodified as authoritarianism, militarism, and neofascism. In general, the patriarchy and the fate of Camila O'Gorman are harbingers of a long line of victims of political persecutions, national reorganizations, and dirty wars against alleged subversion.

Bemberg's film is a strictly historical narrative. It provides a careful and convincing recreation of the feel of life in Buenos Aires in the 1840s. Telling Camila's story in no way deviates from the conventions of films recounting the fate of star-struck lovers. The filmic language of *Camila*, in fact, comes on many occasions close to pure soap opera in the effort to provoke an emotional response from the audience and to leave no doubt as to the authentic human story being told. A significant component of narrative verisimilitude in Western societies is the assurance that what is being told is a "true story," and Bemberg's use of what has become a legendary figure in Argentina is designed to have a mass audience appeal. At the same time, Bemberg's film establishes no direct link with contemporary Argentine social history. There is no overt suggestion of an allegorical interpretation of Camila's fate, no specific way in which it is an example of a social and moral authoritarianism that has cast its long shadow over the years in a way that can serve to explain the detentions, tortures, and disappearances of individuals during recent military governments.

Yet, of course, this is precisely how *Camila* has come to be seen, and given Bemberg's filmic production as a whole, it is unreasonable to believe that she could have any objection to such associations. The bases of these associations are many, beginning with the righteous terror of the Rosas regime, which sought legitimacy in themes of returning to the authentic Hispanic/Argentine values, the defense of the family and moral principles, and the imperative for the public display of symbols in support of the authoritarian leader. Bemberg is very effective in providing visual correlatives of the trappings of terror: the mandatory display of the color red, which symbolized the blood of Rosas's enemies (which are, of course, also the enemies of the state); the hordes of thugs who enforced the dictator's version of law, public order, and moral decency in sadistic ways that prefigure modern technological torture and

extermination; and the body language of oppression and terrified deport-
ment, such as the angry grimaces Camila's father assumes in his attempts to
make her conform, the thunderous invocations of moral convention of the
agents of order, and the sly smiles of cynical and complicitous collaborators
who know perfectly well how reality can be molded to match political expediency. *Camila* is a film of impeccable narrative texture, and every detail
is strictly calculated to reinforce the director's vision of the toll taken on
human emotional integrity exerted by oppressive tyranny, especially when
that tyranny shrouds itself in moral superiority.

Camila's story is outrageous, both in the girl's sexual aggressiveness, which
breaks with norms of feminine decency, and in her lack of compunction in
setting her sights on seducing an unwary priest. Ladislao is also an agent of
the patriarchy. The complicity of the Catholic Church with the regime is
made clear on several occasions, especially in its acquiescing with the decision
to execute Camila despite her pregnancy. This point is an important one
because the Church's position, very strongly maintained in Argentina to the
present day, is that abortion is murder. However, in the film's view, Camila's
execution, which is also the "abortion" of her child, is justified on the
grounds of political expediency. Even when Ladislao violates his vow of cel-
ibacy by having sexual relations with Camila and his vow of obedience by
running away with her, he is shown to be weak and unable to rise in the end
to the challenge of Camila's transgressive behavior. The way in which Ladislao is subservient to Camila's will and passion is made clear from the fact
that it is he rather than Camila who is the object of the sexual gaze. Both
actors are physically attractive (Susú Pecoraro, who is Argentine, and Imanol
Arias, who is Spanish), but, like a good feminist director, Bemberg displays
Arias's body rather than Pecoraro's, and she invites the spectator to accept
the legitimacy of Ladislao's being an object of desire for Camila, despite his
status as a priest. Throughout the final segment of the film, approximately
the last thirty minutes, Camila continues to assert her character, despite the
depths of despair to which Ladislao sinks. As she considers plans to escape
from Rosas's troops, the best he can do is to go to church to pray for his
soul. Bemberg may be betraying her commitment to Argentine/Hispanic
anticlericalism, but the important point is the contrast in the behavior of the
two lovers, which makes it obvious why Camila became a national legend,
while no one remembers poor, pitiful Ladislao.

Like *La historia oficial*, *Camila* is marked by a considerable investment in
the codes of the Hollywood film. Photography and sound are of impressive
quality, and Bemberg has made use of the best artistic talent Argentina has
to offer. In fact, Camila's brutal and self-serving father is played by Héctor

Alterio, who later played the sinister businessman in Puenzo's film. However, in the case of *Camila*, there is a special point to be made about the lustrous quality of the film as a visual product. This has to do with the juxtaposition between the rich quality of Camila's life as a daughter of the oligarchy and the bestiality of Rosas's reign of terror centered on the livid blood-red symbols of the tyranny, which makes the representation of violence that much more shocking as are the ruptures of the details of illusory privilege. Clearly, historical narratives are primarily of interest because they tell us something about contemporary life. What is seductive in historical narrative is something that is either of a whole with what we are now or in some way prefigures what we have become. For Bemberg and for similar filmmaking in Argentina during the period of institutional redemocratization, the imperative was as much to provide critical and analytical interpretations of the recently concluded period of military tyranny as it was to propose ways of understanding how that tyranny is not an isolated event in the nation's social history. Furthermore, from a specifically feminist point of view, writers, dramatists, and other cultural producers, with whom Bemberg associated, have been particularly concerned to provide interpretations of patriarchal authoritarianism, not just as it affected women, but how it has established a climate of oppression that affects everyone, even when women may be its "privileged" victims.

A FUNNY DIRTY LITTLE WAR

Much more in the paradigmatic masculinist tradition of Argentine filmmaking is Héctor Olivera's *No habrá más penas ni olvido* (A funny dirty little war, 1983). This tradition is masculine in the sense that it deals with social history from essentially the male point of view—women's history is absent, assumed to be subservient to male history, or implied to be one and the same thing. It is masculine also in the sense that, despite the appearance of female protagonists and even female stars, the male presence in the film is dominant and, indeed, overwhelming. In the typical masculine film, the dominant presence of men with a particularly narrow range of social identities is not only overwhelming from a feminist point of view, but from perspectives that include other social categories, such as regional identity, and erotic identity, class identity, generational identity, and the like. Argentina has few art films on gays and none on lesbians, the elderly, children, or rural settings except for those that are important to metropolitan concerns.

The main plot line of *No habrá más penas ni olvido* is a direct allusion to the internal conflicts of the Peronista party in Argentina. A conflict in a small rural town between different groups, essentially the left-wing and right-wing groups that vied for control of the party (always weighted toward the right) during the early 1970s, becomes a full-blown armed conflict between rival factions. The film, based on Osvaldo Soriano's 1980 novel of the same name, is grim black humor because it combines the laughable absurdity of the bases of the conflict with the reality that people are tortured and assassinated, major property destruction occurs, and deep social wounds are inflicted. Olivera's allegory of the major political issues in Argentine social history is especially brilliant because he takes the conflict down to the very personal level by grounding it in the daily lives of individuals. Moreover, by transferring the conflict from the heady context of the grand stage of national events in Buenos Aires to the scrabbly arena of an otherwise entirely forgettable town lost in the vast plains of the Pampas, Olivera succeeds in demonstrating how such ideological conflicts are driven by what is ultimately trivial and also how such trivialities, when elevated to the scale of momentous political truths, impact so disastrously on the pathetic lives of common people.

On another level, Olivera's allegory is not just about the internal power struggles of the Peronista party and the government it put in power in 1973. Rather, the film is primarily of interest, even for an Argentine audience, because of the fratricide that has characterized Argentine history during the past sixty years, since the first military takeover in 1930. Politics, of course, always means the often brutal give-and-take between conflicting beliefs. It is natural to expect that a change in government will lead to structural changes in society when the political philosophies of different governments circulate through the state apparatus and social and cultural components are affected to one degree or another by it. However, Argentina has had three major military coups since 1955, with three military dictators between 1966 and 1973 and four between 1976 and 1983. In 1973, there were four presidents: the military man who turned the government over to the Peronistas and the three civilians who followed, the last of whom was Perón. Finally, 1982 saw a senseless war between Argentina and England over the Malvinas, an event that totally discredited the military and allowed for the return of democracy in 1983. However, the war also brought political instability to Argentina, especially in its international relations, and the casualties were added to those of the Dirty War. The Malvinas conflict also occasioned an outburst of jingoism that, if it now seems to be ridiculous, fed monstrously into the reactionary nationalism of the dictatorships.

It is this quality of monstrosity that Olivera really captures so well in his film. Basically, a series of misunderstandings that derive from obeisance to trivial political ideologies results in a violent escalation of conflict that ultimately avails itself of the full arsenal of the military exercise of power: the

town of Colonia Vela turns into a battlefield in which thirty years of Argentine history are reenacted, including the torture of prisoners, the confrontation between armed vehicles, and the bombardment of civilians. When
Cevino, who earns a living piloting a small crop duster, dumps a load of pig
manure on the combatants, the film makes its most eloquent statement about
recent Argentine political history, its agents, and its administration. Olivera
made the film in the context of the victory in 1983 of the Radical Civic
Union against the Peronista candidate, and there are those spectators who
view it as a commentary on the national tragedy of the return to power of
Perón and the Peronistas, especially in view of both the earlier Peronista
governments and the internal conflicts during the twenty years it took Perón
to return to Argentina. The brief redemocratization of Argentina in the mid-
1970s was, in view of the violence recorded by this film, hardly any improve-
ment over military tyranny. To be sure, this sounds a bit like an official story,
since Olivera made his film in the context, and with the support, of the
government of the Radical Civic Union which assumed the presidency at the
end of 1983. The Peronista party and the Union have long been (aside from
the armed forces and the Church, which has traditionally supported the
armed forces) the principal opponents in Argentine politics.

But, then, what is it that could be analyzed about *A Funny Dirty Little
War* beyond the exact details of Peronista misfortunes in the 1970s or as a
farce regarding the status of human rights in Latin America? I would propose
that what is of dominant interest in the film is the question of the consequences of ideological conflict. Ideology—political, religious, or social—
structures the meanings of our lives and provides us with the fundamental
principles for constructing our horizons of meaning. For a society like Argentina, the juxtaposition of ideological positions is less between differing
political positions, although one would certainly argue that on a fairly basic
level of political life this is what is involved. Rather, the perceived differences
cast themselves in larger terms than partisan disagreement. What is involved
is the disagreement between the possibility of any social pact in the first place
versus a resignation to something like a perpetual political bloodletting. Under such circumstances, accords, pacts, and the like are quite simply impossible. Thus, Argentine society is not characterized so much by political
instability and lack of respect for individual rights, but rather instability is a
form of dominant social structure that only makes it appear that more human
rights abuses occur than in a more "politically civilized" society.

No habrá más penas ni olvido tends toward the farcical because it turns on
the representation of the necessary failure of social pacts and the inevitable
irrationality of opposing political positions. Disengaging from the concern

of the period in either defending canonical Peronismo or in advocating a renovation of Peronismo through the inclusion of the (new) left, Olivera projects the incapability of Peronismo ever to provide an acceptable political base for Argentina. Its internal contradictions are simply too great, and therefore it is not a question of Peronismo versus other political parties, but rather social chaos versus legitimate partisan politics. Since Argentina basically has been ruled by Peronismo for fifty years, either directly by a member of the Peronista party or in opposition to Peronismo. And since Peronismo in the 1970s—and perhaps again in the 1990s—is a perfect example of how what is forgotten in history often returns in terrifying new versions (whether with the military or any partisan position that believes Argentina must overcome its Peronista heritage), Olivera is able to use the internal dissention within the party, which is, once again, the consequence of its unresolvable internal contradictions, as a figure of the unresolvability of Argentine social life.

Olivera's film is very good, which is why it has had a certain level of favorably critical reception outside Argentina. An inquiry into how the film was received and interpreted outside Argentina neither detracts from the quality of Olivera's filmmaking nor questions the authenticity of his social and political interpretation. Rather, it concerns how the viewing of films from Latin America, and particularly from a society like Argentina that seems to be so much a part of the capitalist hegemony and yet so much a part of a subalternized Latin America, cannot be simply a matter of a direct and unmediated meaning. Knowledge of the actual historical events being represented is not really the issue. Knowledge of the way in which whatever knowledge the spectator possesses of the events is interpreted, however, is very much the issue, which also includes how the spectator constructs a meaning for those events on the basis of a whole network of beliefs and prejudices about supposedly non-Western societies.

JORGE POLACO

The three films discussed up to this point are all available with English subtitles, and all have been reviewed in English-language sources; moreover, they have been the object of extensive critical analyses. Jorge Polaco's *Diapasón* (Tuning fork, filmed in 1985 but not released until 1986) has not appeared in the U.S. market. However, Polaco is, in the judgment of many, Argentina's most important director to have emerged in the last ten years, and *Diapasón* is one of the most controversial, recently made Argentine films.

Polaco's film is difficult for a number of reasons. It seems, at first, to be a typical flashback narrative—in which an opening sequence jumps back to an event in the past that is then the basis for a forward-moving narrative—until we reach the moment in which the flashback took place. The narrative is difficult to piece together because it does not move forward in a straight line after the flashback. Moreover, there is the sense that segments of the film have been cut out (an eerie reminder of how many films during the dictatorship were fragmented not by the director's auteurist design but by the censor's suppressions), which means that the spectator must make an enormous interpretive effort. Individual scenes and sequences are constructed with enormous complexity, but they are disjointed in such a way that the spectator must relate them together through an act of semantic calculus, so to speak.

The film is also difficult in its representation of violence, which involves not only the issue of accepting such representation, but of relating it to a process of interpretation. The title of the film refers to a recurring motif of the tuning fork as part of the cultivation of music. However, in a symbolic sense, it refers to the way in which individuals are "tuned" in order to make them fit into society. More specifically, it refers to the male protagonist's efforts to make the middle-aged woman he has taken as a lover conform to his notions of femininity, sexual relations, and suitable companionship. Although the film in this sense is an examination of violence against women in forcing them to conform to a masculine definition of womanhood and punishing them when they do not fulfill the conditions set for them, Polaco also shows the resistance used by the female protagonist to challenge her "mentor" before she finally leaves him. Although the sense of violent training and correction are disturbing, there is nevertheless a strong vein of grotesque humor in the film that makes it an extremely fascinating work. The Argentine film code, which closely resembles that of the United States, nevertheless is fairly open as to what it will permit minors to see. *Diapasón*, however, bears the most restrictive classification, and it is available only to those who are eighteen and older.

ELISEO SUBIELA

Eliseo Subiela is a contemporary filmmaker who has received international attention, and his *El lado oscuro del corazón* (The dark side of the heart, 1992) took major prizes at both the Montreal and Biarritz film festivals. The story concerns a poet who seeks a woman who can fly (a term meant to be taken literally in a whimsical way, but also her ability to be deeply erotic). As he pursues his ideal, he is constantly haunted by the figure of Death, a female image that keeps bringing him "back down to earth" with respect to the limitations on human aspiration. The backdrop of the film is a reprise of the artistic ferment of the Argentina of the 1960s, a period prior to the 1966 neofascist coup d'état that has assumed legendary, even mythic proportions in the national consciousness. Subiela undermines this idealization of the 1960s by refloating in the film, in a highly critical manner, many of the motifs that continue to circulate in Argentine society: the privileged suffering poet, liberation of the human spirit through art, transcendent erotic fulfillment, woman as poetic ideal, woman as the bane of man, the prostitute as the quintessence of social margination.

Subiela's film is also highly poetic in the sense that many inventive filmic codes are used, including departures from naturalistic color, soft camera shots, and flights of fantasy. The material reality of the city of Buenos Aires (and Montevideo) is there, but foregrounded details are distorted from a norm of strict documentary realism in order to underscore profound human feelings. There is a very "French" feel to Subiela's film, which makes it particularly appealing to sophisticated Argentine audiences who pride themselves on their need for something other than Hollywood fare and Latin American variations on the imperative of hard-hitting social realism. By contrast to Polaco's grotesque representation of sexual politics, Subiela, in the tradition of the continuing Argentine commitment to psychoanalysis (even if more the Jacques Lacan variety now than Freud), strives for a very imaginative symbolization of sexuality. Along with the image of the levitating bodies of an erotically engaged couple, an icon of *El lado oscuro* is a recurring image, against the backdrop of the city, of an enormous sculpture of a phallus on a platform pulled by the artist and his accomplices. When they arrive at the gallery where the sculpture is to be exhibited, the entrance is an appropriately sized vulva. This may serve to represent the sexual drama that is at the core of all social relationships, but it is also an unmistakable sign of the way in which the film is profoundly masculine. Woman, fixed in place (the gallery), exists whether saintly prostitute or dread figure of death, as part of a strictly male fantasy (which, like the phallic sculpture, roams free), and woman has no existence outside of that imagery.

CONCLUSION

Argentine filmmaking gives every indication of continuing to hold a secure place in the spectrum of the country's cultural production. Despite the enormous invasion of American and other foreign films, thanks to the suspension of censorship in 1983 and recent neoliberalist economic policies that encourage imports, dozens of major films are made each year—major in the sense of the talent of the directors, actors, and artistic crews involved and major in the sense of the issues of national concern with which they deal. Neoliberalism has, nevertheless, permitted an increase in quality because it has allowed the importation of photographic and editing equipment that has brought Argentine filmmaking up to an international technological level. Also, while the proliferation of video rentals has meant a decline in movie house attendance and the disappearance of movie houses in many cities and in many neighborhoods of Buenos Aires, a larger percentage of the populace is viewing movies because of the greater access allowed by video. Much of the viewing may be of blockbuster Hollywood films and even of bad American films dumped on the Latin American market, but it also means a greater viewing of Argentine films as well. Finally, the rich history of Argentine filmmaking is readily available on television. Not only is there specific programming of Argentine films, but the enormous range of conventional and cable channels available to most viewers in both the cities and outlying areas means that national films join subbed and subtitled foreign ones as part of a necessary programming staple. All of these factors support the extensive film culture in Argentina and will continue to contribute, along with Argentina's important cultural industry as a whole, to sustaining a first-rate filmmaking industry in that country.

NOTE

1. When I saw the film in July 1985 in Buenos Aires, an elderly woman seated behind me pounded the armrests of her seat as the credits rolled, muttering, "The sons of bitches." I was unable to determine whether she was cursing the military for its abuses or the filmmakers for daring to question the motives and behavior of the de facto government. Of course, I chose to believe the former.

REFERENCES

El cine argentino 1933–1995. CD-ROM. Buenos Aires: Fundación Cinemateca Argentina, 1995.

España, Claudio, comp. *Cine argentino en democracia, 1983–1993.* Buenos Aires: Fondo Nacional de las Artes, 1994.

Foster, David William. *Contemporary Argentine Cinema.* Columbia: University of Missouri Press, 1992.

The Garden of Forking Paths: Argentine Cinema. Edited by John King and Nissa Torrents. London: British Film Institute, 1988.

Marupe, Raúl, and María Alejandra Portela. *Un diccionario de films argentinos.* Buenos Aires: Corregidor, 1995.

6

Literature

SINCE ITS EMERGENCE as an independent republic in the early nineteenth century, Argentina has manifested itself as a nation with an identity crisis. This has been sustained by an almost uninterrupted series of social disruptions characterized by political instability and economic insecurity brought on by the violent clashing of opposing ideologies. Not surprisingly, the national literature has provided an enduring and rather detailed social record of Argentina's struggle to comprehend the national culture and the events that shape it.

Argentina has no significant body of literature from the colonial period such as the famous chronicles of discovery and conquest that are associated with Mexico or Peru, the two principal Spanish viceroyalties. In fact, the territory that now comprises Argentina was considered to be nothing more than hostile and useless outback until the nineteenth century. The one outstanding text from the eighteenth century is *El lazarillo de ciegos caminantes* (The guide for blind wayfarers, 1776), written by Alonso Carrió de la Vandera (1715–1783), popularly known as Concolorcorvo. *El lazarillo* is a pseudoliterary travelogue of the trip between the port of Buenos Aires and Lima, Peru, written following the tradition of the picaresque, with a great deal of humor and irony and some rather scathing criticism of the government. What makes Concolorcorvo's text so important today is the vast amount of information to be found in it regarding the details of colonial life such as the cost of living, the availability of basic supplies, and the customs, flora, and fauna of the region. *El lazarillo* is more often categorized within Peruvian literature, but it does provide one of the most significant records of life in colonial Argentina.

Argentine literature, then, really does not begin to materialize into a recognizable body of writing until the nineteenth century, when enough texts reflective of the historic/political circumstances of the emerging republic began to be produced. This early literature was mainly written by statesmen and politicians and used as a forum for debating and disseminating political agendas. In spite of earlier foundational texts written by such individuals, the first true generation of writers appears in the late nineteenth century and is known as the Generation of 1880, also called the gentlemen-writers. The authors who comprised the Generation of 1880 were elite, high-profile, Liberal leaders and intellectuals, whose goal was to transform Argentina into a European-style nation, which concomitantly meant the rejection of Hispanic tradition and ideals, and which laid the foundation for subsequent ideological battles regarding the very essence of *argentinidad*, or how the nation was to be defined.

Modernism, a literary movement that lasted from about 1880 to 1910, also shaped Argentine literary trends. Modernism was the first truly Latin-American literary movement and Argentina was at the center of it. As a kind of response to the aesthetic and even exaggerated artistry of Modernism was the literature of social realism, written mostly between 1930 and 1950. The literature of this movement is defined by its commitment to social justice and is largely ideologically informed by such international influences as the Russian Revolution, the rise of communism, and Marxism. The years of Peronism, from 1943 to 1955 when Juan Domingo and Eva Perón took the country by storm, generated an immense literary response both in favor of and against the ideology of Peronism. The only historical circumstance to produce a larger body of writing, which can be identified specifically as having come about as a cultural response to it, is the military dictatorship of 1976–1983, known as the Proceso de Reorganización Nacional (Process of National Reorganization). This body of writing is unique not only in its vastness, written by authors living in exile and within the country, but also for its particular metaphorical nature, which was derived from the need to avoid censorship while at the same time speaking out against the atrocities committed by the military. Postdictatorship literature continued throughout the 1980s to provide a sociocultural record of the period of the Proceso. The literature of the 1990s has been influenced by the neoliberalism of the Menem government as well as the general globalization of Argentine culture.

ESTEBAN ECHEVERRÍA

Esteban Echeverría (1805–1851), a leading statesman, was one of the founding figures of Argentina and its literature in the nineteenth century, in spite of the fact that his literary corpus is quite limited. His political essays make up the majority of his writing. Echeverría was raised as a member of the privileged Argentine upper class. He resided in Europen and studied at the Sorbonne, and his literary style adhered closely to French and English romanticism.

As a literary author, Echeverría is known primarily for two texts. The first is his 1837 narrative poem *La cautiva* (The captive woman). It is the tale of María, a white woman held captive by Indians, and Brian, the hero who comes to her rescue. What makes the poem so interesting is that María is a strong romantic heroine who actually ends up carrying her partner. In contrast, Brian is essentially emasculated by repeated failures and defeats that serve to highlight his impotence when faced with the brutality of the primitive environment of the interior. In this way, Echeverría foredates Domingo Faustino Sarmiento's civilization/barbarism equation (discussed in the following section) and provides in Brian a metaphor for the impotence of any man who attempts to confront the dictator Juan Manuel de Rosas. In the end, both characters succumb to the inhospitable terrain.

Echeverría is best remembered for his classic text "El matadero" (The slaughterhouse), first published in 1871, twenty years after the author's death. It is generally agreed that Echeverría wrote the text sometime between 1839 and 1840. "El matadero" is difficult to characterize in terms of literary genre. Critics have classified it as a short story, an essay, and a local color sketch. It is most frequently referred to as the first short story in Spanish America, at least as a precursor to the genre. More important than what it is, however, is the message it conveys. "El matadero" is in no uncertain terms an allegory of the sociocultural circumstances under Rosas's regime wherein the slaughterhouse represents the nation and the space for the conflict between civilization and barbarism to be played out in graphic descriptions of brutal violence. The first part of the text is mostly descriptive; the author places the action temporally in the year 183 . . . (probably 1839) during Lent. There is clear criticism of both the Church and the government, expressed through a clever discourse imbued with Paschal, or Easter, symbology on the importance of meat in the Argentine diet.

However, the political thrust of the story comes later on with the frenzied slaughter of the cattle. By setting his story in the slaughterhouse, Echeverría not only signals the benefits reaped by the beef industry under the Rosas regime, but also the violent repression exercised by the dictator. Moreover, it is readily apparent how Rosas used both beef and brutality to manipulate his followers. In the story, Rosas's ostensibly charitable act of giving away free meat to the desperate crowd is undermined by the way in which the scene is depicted. Echeverría describes the slaughter as an appalling spectacle of savagery in which a depraved, bloodthirsty mob is worked into a frenzy and people fight over entrails and viscera like a pack of mad dogs. Such is the delirium of the crowd that almost no one notices when a rampaging bull snaps the rope to which it was tethered and decapitates a young boy. The crowd chases the bull down the street where it is eventually cornered and killed.

Here enters the young Unitarian dandy on his horse. The crowd, still excited by the recent kill, knocks the political rival from his mount and begins to give him the same treatment as they gave the bull. He is taken back to the slaughterhouse, where he is humiliated, tortured, sodomized, and eventually dies. The parallels between the bull and the Unitarian are clear; the savagery of Rosas and his followers knows no bounds and promises to eradicate anything and anyone who stands in opposition. Echeverría's biased tale about the demise of the Unitarian hero and his outspoken opposition to the Rosas regime set the stage for one of the defining leitmotifs, or dominant recurring themes, of Argentine literature: the binary opposition between civilization and barbarism.

DOMINGO FAUSTINO SARMIENTO

The educator, diplomat, statesman, and eventual president Domingo Faustino Sarmiento (1811–1888) set the foundation for what would come to be one of the defining elements of the national character. Sarmiento was a staunch and outspoken opponent of the nineteenth-century dictator Juan Manuel de Rosas, whose brutal regime lasted from 1835 to 1852. Sarmiento spent a major portion of the Rosas dictatorship exiled in Chile, where he wrote his most famous works. In 1848 he published *Civilización i barbarie. Vida de Juan Facundo Quiroga, aspecto físico, costumbres y hábitos de la República Argentina*, translated into English as *Life in the Argentine Republic in the Days of the Tyrants, or Civilization and Barbarism* by Mary Mann, the wife of American educator Horace Mann. Sarmiento had established a strong friendship with Horace Mann during a stay in the United States, a country he admired with great passion and believed Argentina would do well to emulate. He perceived American puritanism to have many social benefits, and he viewed the United States as a model for what Argentina could become. Of course, he received much criticism for his exuberant support and veneration of the North American country, as well as for his radical stance concerning issues of race. In brief, he was staunchly anti-indigenist, supporting the virtual extermination of the country's native populations, and he regarded European immigration as the best method to bring civility to Argentina.

Popularly known as *Facundo*, Sarmiento's text consists of a diagnosis of the ills of Argentine society under Rosas and prescribes a remedy. His analysis of the sociopolitical situation of the country is based on the dichotomy of civilization versus barbarism. This conflict is played out in the text in a variety of binarisms presented in black-and-white terms of good against evil, man versus nature, European versus indigenous/gaucho, centralism versus federalism, urban versus rural culture.

The book, which is written as a prose essay but with some novelistic features, is divided into three sections. The first part is a straightforward presentation of the problems that plague the young nation. From the very beginning, Sarmiento pits civilized Buenos Aires against the great expanses of land: "El mal que aqueja a la República Argentina es la extensión; el desierto que la rodea por todas partes" (The evil that afflicts the Argentine Republic is the vast expanses of land, the desert that surrounds it from all points). One of the most famous aspects of *Facundo* is the author's characterization of the different types of gauchos that inhabit the "uncivilized" interior of the country, which he provides so that the reader will recognize the qualities of the caudillos, or military dictators, that populate the text. The third section outlines a progressive social program for the future.

The second section, which traditionally has been studied as the most literary portion of the text, relates the life of Juan Facundo Quiroga, a caudillo whom Rosas appointed to govern Sarmiento's home province of San Juan in northeastern Argentina. The author utilizes the figure of Quiroga to illustrate the barbarism endemic to the interior of the country and compares it to the systematic, institutionalized barbarism of Rosas. The dictator is presented as being the evolved result of the uncontrolled barbaric behavior that has now become an organized political force that threatens the civility of the capital and very future of the nation.

Sarmiento's text stirred up great controversy when it first appeared, and it has since become one of the basic texts in Argentine social history. It continues to be the subject of new analyses and re-readings, which is also true of Sarmiento's many other writings. It is unlikely that the author realized at the time just how long-lasting and far-reaching his binarism would become and to what extent it would eventually inform the Argentine social makeup.

The legacy of *Facundo* is evident in subsequent classic works such as *Radiografía de la pampa* (X-ray of the Pampa, 1933) and *La cabeza de Goliat* (Goliath's head, 1940) by Ezequiel Martínez Estrada (1895–1964) and *Historia de una pasión argentina* (History of an Argentine Passion, 1937) by Eduardo Mallea (1903–1982). One of the most fascinating contemporary texts to undertake the challenge of Argentine collective self-definition is Marcos Aguinis's *Un país de novela: viaje hacia la mentalidad de los argentinos* (A fictional country: Voyage into the Argentine mentality, 1988). Aguinis examines the country from a personal perspective, using the narrative structure of a travelogue. The author does not attempt to retell Argentine history. Rather, he embarks on a voyage of discovery through the history of attitudes and influences that have contributed to the evolution of the Argentine national character since before colonial times.

José Hernández

The definitive work of Argentine literature was written in the nineteenth century by José Hernández (1834–1886), the son of moderate-income parents who often traveled and left the young Hernández in the care of his aunt. Because of a pulmonary condition that doctors felt was exacerbated by the damp city climate, Hernández spent much of his youth on the vast cattle ranches his father administered for Rosas. There he came into close contact with and learned the ways of the gaucho ranch hands. As was common at the time, Hernández eventually became a political figure cum writer. He was recruited by Rosas's Federalist army to fight the Unitarians. When Rosas was defeated, he fell into disfavor with President Sarmiento and was forced to live a period of exile in neighboring Uruguay. Hernández is known for his lengthy epoch poem *El gaucho Martín Fierro* (1872) and its sequel, *La vuelta de Martín Fierro* (1879). *Martín Fierro* followed a tradition of gauchesque literature in the River Plate written in the late nineteenth century by such authors as Bartolomé Hidalgo (1788–1822), Hilario Ascasubi (1807–1875), Estanislao del Campo (1834–1880), and Antonio Lussich (1848–1928). Hernández's predecessors in the genre generally used the figure of the gaucho to satirize the political controversies of the time. Hernández was one of the first to create a true-to-life depiction of the gaucho, just as this legendary figure of the Pampas was beginning to disappear. *Martín Fierro* is often regarded to be the finest work of Spanish American romanticism. It almost immediately became a best-seller and was one of the most widely distributed literary works in all of Spanish America. It became an instant classic of Argentine literature and endures today as the standard literary work of Argentina, similar to Miguel de Cervantes's *Don Quixote* in Spanish literature. *Martín Fierro* embodies Argentine identity and contains the essence of the national soul, at least as it is perceived in romantic, mythological terms.

El gaucho Martín Fierro narrates the tribulations of the eponymous hero who lives as a renegade on the margins of a society caught up in a rapid process of modernization that has left no room for his kind. Fierro is a *payador*, a gaucho minstrel, who sings his story, and he begins by relating a series of personal calamities: he has lost his home, his family, and his livelihood. In despair and disgust over a government policy that has completely disrupted his life and stripped him of all that was most dear to him, Fierro becomes a type of desperado who eventually rejects the European ideals of civilization and goes to live with the Pampa Indians. The character Sergeant Cruz, who initially was sent to bring Fierro in, defects from the army and becomes his companion. That these two men would rather live among the Indians than as part of the society being developed in Buenos Aires constituted a strong political statement. The first part of the poem, also known as the *Ida* (Departure), represents the rejection of official policy and the failure of the government to integrate fully all members of society.

The publication seven years later of *La vuelta de Martín Fierro* (The return of Martin Fierro) illustrates Hernández's own change of perspective regarding national policy. The second part represents a reconciliation of sorts on the part of Fierro with the authorities. The character is less rebellious and more philosophical, and he is joined by a chorus of marginal individuals who are coming to terms, if reluctantly, with the inevitable evolution of society. A significant part of the second half deals with the reunion of Fierro with his two sons and with the son of Cruz. *La vuelta* succeeds in demonstrating the necessary demise of the traditional gaucho, but it also romanticizes the nomadic plainsman and creates a figure of mythic proportions that has become the heroic symbol of the Argentine psyche. *Martín Fierro* stands alone as a classic for its melding of authentic gaucho speech, humor, and philosophy, and for the tremendous lyricism in the portrayal of nature and the human characters. Hernández's poem has been praised by subsequent giants of Argentine literature such as Leopoldo Lugones and Jorge Luis Borges. Lugones gave a series of lectures in 1913 at the Teatro Odeón in Buenos Aires on *Martín Fierro*. These were later collected and published in book form as *El payador* in 1916. In his effort to prove that *Martín Fierro* was undoubtedly the epic song of Argentina, Lugones sought to establish a direct link between Hernández's poem and the epic poetry of ancient Greece.

At the turn of the century, Buenos Aires was the undisputed center of the modernist movement in Spanish South America (Mexico City was the focal point in the Northern Hemisphere). It attracted the best writers from the Spanish-speaking world, including the Nicaraguan-born poet Rubén Darío (1867–1916), who together with Leopoldo Lugones (1874–1938) made Buenos Aires the capital of the modernist movement in its second phase during the first decade of the twentieth century. Argentina had emerged from the strife of the nineteenth century to become one of the wealthiest, most modernized, and most sophisticated countries of Latin America. In fact, Buenos Aires resembled a European capital more than a South American one. Modernism constituted the first truly Spanish American literary movement, insofar as it came about as an independent reaction to the nineteenth-century romanticism inherited from European models. Modernist writers, most of whom were poets, sought the creation of a new literary language characterized by unusual rhymes, synesthesia (sensory confusion), and new rhythmical and metrical combinations. This literature was typified by insistence on beauty, ornamentalism, and classical or mythological symbolism. While it was a reaction against the perceived stodginess of romantic literature, it also reflected a great deal of apprehension toward the rapid industrialization of society and belied a distrust in the dubious virtues of science and technology.

LEOPOLDO LUGONES

Leopoldo Lugones is without doubt Argentina's greatest modernist author and one of the finest in Latin America. As a poet he gained almost instant fame with his 1897 collection *Las montañas del oro* (The golden mountains). Because of the poet's use of exotic imagery, embellished language, and outlandish metaphors the volume was praised for being innovative and for exalting the role of the poet within society. The poem's modernist aspects are also to be found in the way Lugones skillfully incorporated urban, scientific, and technological images of a new age into the verses. In *Los crepúsculos del jardín* (Garden twilights, 1905), Lugones continued his experimentation with lexical and rhythmic poetic patterns. This second collection of poetry is considered to be one of the texts that most thoroughly exemplifies the conventions of Spanish American modernism.

Lugones was as skilled a prose writer as he was a poet. In 1905 he published his first prose work, *La guerra gaucha* (The gaucho war), which is a remarkable text in many ways. It is composed of twenty-three interrelated episodes that narrate the struggles for independence in northern Argentina. The stories are told from the perspective of the gaucho soldiers, and in particular the adventures of Martín Güemes, a nineteenth-century gaucho hero. The narrative is highly complex in its use of metaphor and lyricism, and is known especially for its excessive use of arcane vocabulary. The text is so complex that it prompted Jorge Luis Borges to comment on the convoluted, baroque style of prose. In spite of these difficulties, the novel has enjoyed numerous reprintings and was made into a film.

Lugones soon revealed himself to be a master of the short story, too, with the publication of his *Las fuerzas extrañas* (Strange forces) in 1906. His narrative in this second prose volume reveals a significant change in style, far less burdened with the exaggerated syntactic and lexical entanglements of *La guerra gaucha*. The stories also diverge thematically to focus on elements of the supernatural, the strange forces of nature, the occult, and science. The volume contains twelve stories supplemented by a treatise on cosmogony. The attention to the supernatural in the stories reveals another aspect of modernism. Seances, consultations with psychic mediums, and the study of theosophy and the Kabbalah were all popular activities in Buenos Aires at the turn of the century. Likewise, foreign authors, such as Edgar Allan Poe and Guy de Maupassant, were widely read and assimilated by modernist writers. The hair-raising tales of *Las fuerzas extrañas* gained Lugones a reputation as a master of suspense and horror. Cruel deaths inevitably befell his characters as a type of cosmic retribution for having meddled with the forces of nature, a fate that reflected society's angst over the technologization of culture. His stories were often presented as being based on true occurrences and included such fictional documentation as diary entries, fragments of lost manuscripts, lengthy theoretical hypotheses, and scientific data of the author's own invention.

Lugones was placed in charge of organizing the cultural commemorations for the first centenary of independence from Spain in 1910. He offered his own *Odas seculares* (Centennial odes) as one of the contributions. *Odas* is significant not only for the occasion for which it was written but, more important, because it marks a change in direction for the poet himself. For the first time, Lugones based his poetry on specifically Argentine themes. The ten separate poems that constitute the volume all portray the people, places, and history of Argentina. The volume marks the beginning of Lugones's gradual personal evolution from the socialism of his early years to the nationalist, indeed overtly fascist, stance of his later years. Lugones seemingly foretold of his death at his own hand in his last novel, *El ángel de la muerte* (The angel of death, 1926), which treats the topic of suicide at length.

ALBERTO GERCHUNOFF

Alberto Gerchunoff (1884–1950) was one of the authors whom Lugones commissioned to write a book as part of the centenary celebration. Gerchunoff, who was born in Proskuroff, Russia, emigrated to Argentina with his family in 1889. He spent his early years in the Jewish agricultural colonies established by Baron Maurice de Hirsch in the province of Entre Ríos. He later moved to Buenos Aires, where he became the first, and one of the few,

Jewish writers to gain acceptance into mainstream Argentine literature. His writing has become normalized into the literary canon to such a point that he does not represent a problem, as a Jewish writer, within the predominately Hispano-Catholic literary tradition—as do many other Jewish writers. Gerchunoff consciously and energetically engaged in a lifelong process of forming an identity as a nonthreatening Argentine of Jewish descent. Central to this process was his insistence on language, in this case Spanish, as the vehicle for the construction of a cultural and personal identity.

Gerchunoff is the author of over twenty volumes of fiction and nonfiction prose, but he is most remembered for his 1910 *Los gauchos judíos* (The Jewish gauchos of the Pampas). The text, which can be read as a series of interrelated short stories or as a novel, is considered to be the cornerstone of Jewish literature in Latin America. The work, autobiographical in nature, relates the experience of the Jewish immigrants in their new country. Several episodes relate directly to the author's own life, such as the murder of his father by a drunken gaucho.

Contemporary criticism of Gerchunoff's text has focused on the author's overly idyllic representation of the Jewish experience in Argentina, which glosses over the often extreme prejudice suffered and endured by Jews. It is understandable that, at the time, Gerchunoff may have been more concerned about gaining acceptance than risking alienation from his peers. He also truly believed in a very literal sense that Argentina was the Promised Land for the beleaguered Eastern European and Russian Jews who sought refuge from persecution in the Old World. The legacy of Gerchunoff as a pioneer Jewish author cannot be ignored. He led the way for subsequent Jewish writers in Argentina for at least three generations.

THE FLORIDA GROUP AND THE BOEDO GROUP

The 1920s was a time of innovation and intense activity in literary circles in Buenos Aires. It was during this time that literature began to be considered seriously as a profession and not merely as a pastime, although this sentiment had began to be formed with the modernist writers. A literary avant-garde was under way which sought a different vision of the form and function of literature. What direction this should take, and especially what was the role of literature, was perceived quite differently among writers.

One group of writers that rallied around the newly formed literary journal *Martín Fierro* (1924–1927) concentrated on finding new modes of expression and exploring new themes. They took an essentially aesthetic approach to literature. Writers in this group included Oliverio Girondo (1891–1967),

Jorge Luis Borges (1899–1986), Macedonio Fernández (1874–1952), and Ricardo Güiraldes (1886–1927). This band of writers, collectively known as the Florida group, was associated with the posh area of Buenos Aires known for high society gatherings and its upscale cultural environment. Because of their close association with the journal, they also were known as the *martín-fierristas*, and for many the Buenos Aires avant-garde literary movement was synonymous with *martínfierrismo*.

Representing the opposite pole of the avant-garde literary spectrum were the Boedo writers. They took their name from the working-class neighborhood from which many of them came or to which they could at least relate. Although they also endeavored to effect a change in literary style, their main purpose was to use and promote literature as a means for social change. As opposed to the Florida writers, who generally came from well-established Creole families, the Boedo group comprised children of immigrants who had grown up with a much different vision of social reality. These proletarian writers included Leónidas Barletta (1902–1975), Roberto Mariani (1892–1946), Elías Castelnuovo (1893–1982), and Alvaro Yunque (pseud. of Arístides Gandolfi Herrero [1889–1982]). The works produced by these authors, primarily narrative, were lacking in terms of polished literary language and textual cohesion. However, what concerned them was the message of the text, not the method. Their works focused on narrating the plight of the worker and the lower classes, and they concentrated on describing in detail the conditions of the work place.

RICARDO GÜIRALDES

Ricardo Güiraldes, a member of the Argentine oligarchy, enjoyed all the luxuries of life this privileged status afforded him. He periodically resided in Paris for extensive lengths of time and he quite literally traveled around the globe. His travels are readily apparent in his works, whether in direct depictions of his adventures or in the influence of foreign movements and authors. As an author himself, Güiraldes had a rather shaky beginning. He aligned himself with the Florida group, but he was not taken very seriously by his fellow writers, and his early works were deemed inferior in style and artistic content. The negative reaction to his first volume of poetry, *El cencerro de cristal* (The crystal cow bell, 1915), prompted Güiraldes, in an act of despair, to throw the remaining copies of the volume down the well at La Porteña, the family ranch. Güiraldes eventually published six works during his lifetime; another eight were published posthumously.

In 1926 Güiraldes published his novel *Don Segundo Sombra*, and it became an instant classic of Argentine literature. The novel, which he worked on for seven years, earned him the prestigious National Literature award and marked the culmination of his career as a writer. The novel has been reprinted innumerable times; it is used as an essential text in virtually all Argentine schools; it has been translated into ten languages; and it was made into a motion picture in 1969.

Don Segundo Sombra is a classic bildungsroman—that is, a novel that narrates the development of the young protagonist into an adult and the process of the character's formation. As a young orphan, Fabio Cáceres is taken under the tutelage of Don Segundo Sombra, a wise old gaucho who becomes the boy's mentor and guides him through his apprenticeship on the rugged Pampas and his initiation into manhood. The eponymous character of the novel was loosely based on Segundo Ramírez, a ranch hand who worked on the Güiraldes family *estancia* (cattle ranch). The novel unfolds through the first-person narration of the adult Cáceres as he recalls his youth and the character-shaping events of his life. By the end of the novel, Fabio Cáceres, now a hardened gaucho, learns the identity of his father from whom he has inherited a large estate and responsibility. His initial reaction is to reject his newfound wealth since it would mean relinquishing the freedom of the lifestyle to which he has become accustomed. Of course, he ultimately decides to forego the gaucho lifestyle and accept the responsibilities of his inheritance. Fabio ends up with the best of both worlds: he has the stalwart character and integrity of the gaucho and the wealth and power of an *estanciero*, which is probably how Güiraldes viewed himself. The novel is replete with detailed descriptions of life on the cattle ranches, the chores and work ethic of the gauchos, and the customs and traditions of country folk, as well as long portions of text devoted to the awesome beauty and power of Nature.

Don Segundo Sombra reveals much about the general sociopolitical milieu of Argentina in the 1920s, specifically from the perspective of the oligarchy. Constructed as an allegory of the country, the novel detail Argentina's rich past and prescribes a future based on ideals of the land. The text seeks a redemption of traditional Argentine identity based on a return to the Creole values of the rural past. This identity was perceived as being seriously threatened by the huge influx of various immigrant groups who could only contaminate the social makeup of the country. *Don Segundo Sombra* is blatant in its conservatism and justification of the position the oligarchy, politically anti-liberal, and highly xenophobic with regard to immigrants. It is very much a novel about men, masculinity, and the perpetuation of patriarchal ideals. Consequently, it is also exceedingly misogynistic in its treatment of the female characters. Undercurrents of machismo, violence, authoritarianism, and eroticism, all revolving around power struggles and death, permeate the novel.

Güiraldes presents an overly romanticized version of the gaucho way of life, glossing over the very demise of the traditional gaucho at the hands of the landed aristocracy to which he belonged. Don Segundo Sombra, as his name suggests, is truly a shadowy figure, an anachronistic ghost from the past. In fact, he is even described by the narrator as being "más una idea que un hombre" (more an idea than a man). He is the epitome of the gaucho, the romanticized reincarnation of Martín Fierro. Güiraldes managed to create a gaucho narrative that effectively portrayed an image of the national character long sought after. *Don Segundo Sombra* was one of the first texts in which authentic rural speech was successfully incorporated into a work that was artistically sound, although the refined, sophisticated language and lyrical realism of Fabio Cáceres renders a false depiction of the real nature of gaucho life. The psychological development of the characters, through which the exalted gaucho heritage is transmitted, constitutes the prime motivation of the narrative. Despite contemporary critical readings of the novel that point to the facile ideological motivations that make up the subtext of the novel, *Don Segundo Sombra* continues to stand the test of time as a classic text of high literary merit.

ROBERTO ARLT

Roberto Arlt (1900–1942) also came to prominence in the 1920s. The son of immigrants, his primary language was German. He had very little formal education and worked at a variety of odd jobs to eke out a living, and he is said to have dabbled with various inventions. He also worked as a secretary to Ricardo Güiraldes who helped and influenced him a great deal. He did eventually become a reporter for the daily *El Mundo* (The world) as well as several other journals and newspapers. While he associated with writers from both the Florida and Boedo groups, he never actually aligned himself with either. In spite of his association with Güiraldes, his life and his work were at a position 180 degrees from his friend.

Arlt published his first novel, *El juguete rabioso* (The rabid toy), in 1926, the same year as Güiraldes's *Don Segundo Sombra*, and he dedicated the novel to Ricardo Güiraldes. If Güiraldes's novel is one of nostalgia and the grandeur of the Argentine nation and people, then Arlt's is its antithesis. *El juguete rabioso* is also a bildungsroman narrative; however, the protagonist Silvio Astier must rely on his own cunning and the lessons learned on the mean streets of Buenos Aires where the novel is set. Arlt also incorporated authentic speech patterns into his narrative in the form of *lunfardo*, or street slang. The novel is replete with descriptions and the sentiments of misery, alienation, poverty, betrayal, and human suffering in general. This was the reality of the immigrant who came in hopes of making it in America, only to realize that the doors were closed to him. Arlt is also one of the first to include an open treatment of homosexuality in Argentine literature in the episode of Astier's encounter with a young hustler in a cheap hotel. Silvio becomes more and more resentful, desperate, and enraged as the narrative progresses and the abyss widens between his aspirations and the real possibilities available to him. Like Arlt himself, the fictional character of his creation tinkers with various inventions hoping to come up with a get-rich-quick scheme. *El juguete rabioso* does not offer a pat ending as does *Don Segundo Sombra*, wherein the hero rides off into the sunset and the world makes sense again. In contrast, Arlt's novel speaks to the failure of Argentina as a nation to integrate newcomers and the resultant devastation meted out on a wide sector of society that exists on the margins of that world envisioned by the oligarchs.

Even though *El juguete rabioso* was a considerable success at the time of publication, Arlt is more often remembered for his *Aguafuertes porteñas*, local-color sketches of contemporary Argentine life that initially appeared in *El Mundo* and were later collected in book form (1933), and for his 1929 novel *Los siete locos* (The seven madmen) and its sequel *Los lanzallamas* (The flame-throwers, 1931). *Los siete locos* is very similar to *El juguete* in its depiction of the characters and the seedy underside of Buenos Aires life. The protagonist is a downtrodden loser named Remo Erdosain who gets caught up in an underground criminal conspiracy after getting fired from his job for embezzlement. His adventures lead the reader on a tour of the dark side of Argentine reality populated by a host of bizarre characters. The overriding sensation produced by the novel is one of angst, especially on the part of Erdosain. The fragmentation of the novel and the disjointed episodes underscore the alienation and general confusion felt by the characters. Although *Los lanzallamas* continues the story of this group of misfits, most criticism has focused on *Los siete locos*. Arlt was also the author of numerous short stories and plays. His reputation today is that of an unsung genius of Argentine literature, and his influence is readily identifiable in the works of many contemporary writers.

VICTORIA OCAMPO

Victoria Ocampo (1890–1979) was born into one of the wealthiest, most influential families in Argentina. She came to be one of the foremost women writers of her generation, and she exercised considerable influence in the literary world through the journal *Sur* (South), which she founded, edited, and financed. The North American writer Waldo Frank is credited with encouraging Ocampo to create *Sur*, which became one of the longest running literary and intellectual journals in Argentine history, enjoying continuous publication from 1931 to 1970. *Sur* reported all aspects of the arts, although it had a strong literary component. It featured translations of foreign authors as well as texts by established and up-and-coming writers from Argentina, and it was responsible for launching the careers of many of the country's most famous authors. It leaned decidedly toward Ocampo's own oligarchic tastes and ideology, though it never officially claimed to take any particular political affiliation. Ocampo herself was vehemently outspoken in her criticism of Juan Perón and Peronism. Ocampo's own works, mainly essays, have enjoyed newfound attention for their feminist viewpoint.

JORGE LUIS BORGES

There is no figure in Argentine literature, and perhaps in all of Latin America, who looms as large as Jorge Luis Borges (1899–1986). He began his literary career as a young poet who returned from Spain in 1921 to initiate the ultraist movement in Argentine literature. Like other avant-garde movements, ultraism was a reaction against the flowery excesses of modernism. It was designed to strip poetic language down to the bare essentials and move beyond (ultra) all forms associated with isms. Although Borges was a leading figure in Buenos Aires literary circles of the 1920s, he reached true prominence during the 1930s and 1940s, attaining the stature of a literary icon in the 1960s. In spite of his prolific career and the true genius of his work, Borges never received the Nobel prize in literature, a source of great consternation for many Argentines who feel that Borges, and by extension Argentina, was served a great injustice.

While Borges was an exceptional poet and a perceptive essayist, his fame rests on his monumental talent as a short story writer. In 1941 Borges published a collection of his stories with the title *El jardín de los senderos que se bifurcan* (The garden of forking paths), which was later rereleased in an expanded version with the title *Ficciones* (1944; the English version retained the original Spanish title). The typical Borges story is characterized by its labyrinthine structure, an ingenious use of metaphor, the insistence on the cyclical nature of human existence, the refutation of the boundaries of time and space, and multiple levels of reality, leaving each story open to diverse interpretations. His stories often seem too packed, however, with information and minutiae, which can overwhelm the reader who more often than not is unable to process such a proliferation of detail or filter the unnecessary from the essential. The reader of Borges, then, must be an active participant in the story, willing to be patient in unraveling the mystery of the text. Borges managed to achieve the universalization of Argentine literature, turning specifically Argentine themes and symbols into metaphors with universal resonance and appeal. This is undoubtedly one of the factors that contributed to his international success. However, Borges did not always ground his stories in Argentine reality. He found fertile ground for his intricate tales of intrigue and mystery in almost every corner of the globe and effectively utilized the traditions of diverse cultures and mythologies to construct his stories. No other Latin American author has come close to garnering the critical attention that Borges has received, with books numbering in the hundreds and articles in the thousands.

JULIO CORTÁZAR

The second monolithic figure of Argentine literature is Julio Cortázar (1914–1984), who also to the dismay of many never became a Nobel laureate. He was the author of several novels, numerous collections of short stories, poetry, essays, and several prose works which deny classification. Like Borges, he was a master of the short story, specifically in the genre of the fantastic. Cortázar was a controversial figure who maintained a high public profile in national and international politics. In 1951, disgusted with the Peronist regime, he left Buenos Aires and traveled to Paris on a scholarship where he took up permanent residence. He never returned to live in Argentina, and in 1981 he acquired French citizenship. In spite of what may be perceived as a rejection of his native country, Cortázar maintained close ties to Argentina and engaged in many debates with other Argentine writers.

Cortázar gained international fame as one of the so-called boom authors from Latin America together with Gabriel García Márquez (b. 1928) of Colombia, Carlos Fuentes (b. 1928) of Mexico, Mario Vargas Llosa (b. 1936) of Perú, and José Donoso (1924–1996) of Chile. Cortázar's novel *Rayuela* (Hopscotch, 1963) is one of the major works of Latin American new narrative, perhaps second only to García Márquez's *Cien años de soledad* (One hundred years of solitude, 1967). Like much of Borges's literature, *Rayuela* requires the active involvement of the reader, who must piece together the sporadic, seemingly unconnected episodes of narrative that bounce back and forth between Buenos Aires and Paris. Moreover, the novel may be read by following a traditional sequential pattern or by following the directions at the end of each chapter to jump to the next, out of numerical sequence, chapter; thus the title of the book refers to the playful, gamelike quality of the narrative. There is no real plot to the novel, which instead consists mainly of the protagonist's (Horacio Oliveira) search for the meaning of life. The structure of the novel itself seems to be what most attracted its readers who eagerly welcomed the novel's unorthodox experimentation in literary form. His other novels never attracted much attention, and his lasting fame relied on his talent for creating perfectly structured short stories.

Cortázar's most memorable stories, which are in the fantastic or neofantastic vein, recall the tales of suspense written by his River Plate predecessors Leopoldo Lugones and Horacio Quiroga (1878–1937). Like those former authors, Cortázar was greatly influenced by Edgar Allan Poe, whose works he translated into Spanish. These stories are often characterized by the presentation of parallel realities or surreal happenings. Typical of this style is his story "La noche boca arriba" (The night face up) in which a man suffers a motorcycle accident on a Buenos Aires street and is taken to the hospital. In his delirium from the anesthetic he dreams he is the victim of an Aztec sacrifice. As the story progresses, the lines between dream state and reality become blurred until both the character and the reader come to the startling realization that the dream was actually the motorcycle accident and the reality is that he is about to be sacrificed in an Aztec ritual. There is also a ludic, or playful, side to Cortázar's fantasies; one example is the story "Carta a una señorita en París" (Letter to a young woman in Paris), in which the narrator vomits live rabbits.

MANUEL PUIG

The postboom era saw the emergence of Manuel Puig (1932–1990) as a major figure in Latin American letters. In spite of the fact that chronologically his works parallel those of the boom writers, he did not begin to receive recognition until after the heyday of the boom receded. Puig was born in the small provincial town of General Villegas, where he spent his boyhood assimilating the mixed messages of foreign and domestic motion pictures shown at the local cinema. He developed an intense interest in cinematography as an art form and pursued film studies at the famous Centro Sperimentale di Cinematografia in Rome. He worked at a variety of odd jobs before he became established as a writer.

His first novel, *La traición de Rita Hayworth* (Betrayed by Rita Hayworth, 1968), was a critical and popular success. One of Puig's lasting contributions is his successful integration of popular culture (film, tangos and boleros, and soap-opera melodrama) into literature, and he was instrumental in blurring the lines between mass culture and so-called serious art. In *La traición de Rita Hayworth*, the residents of a small town go about their daily lives, with the emphasis of the narrative focused on the way in which mass media and mass cultural production influence them and constrain them, particularly with regard to traditional sex roles.

Puig is best known for his 1976 novel *El beso de la mujer araña* (The kiss of the spider woman), which was made into a film and most recently a Broadway production scripted by Terrence McNally. The novel concerns two men who find themselves sharing a prison cell: Valentín, who was arrested for his political activism, and Molina, who was detained for being a homosexual (under the charge of contributing to the corruption of minors). One of the most ingenious elements of the novel is to be found in Molina's retelling to Valentín the plots of six different films. However, the text also provides potent statements on official programs of repression, such as the oppression of political, social, and sexual adversaries by military governments. Puig was one of the first authors to provide consistently a literary space for the subject of homoeroticism and the gay man as a subject. Nevertheless, in concert, his texts speak more directly to issues of sexuality in general and the ways in which sexual freedom of expression is controlled by societal norms and prejudices as well as the exploration of viable, alternate sexual identities.

ALEJANDRA PIZARNIK

Alejandra Pizarnik (1936–1972) also gained a considerable reputation for dealing openly with issues of sexuality and personal identity. She was primarily a poet, although she did compose several prose works. Unlike Puig, who was able to reap the benefits of his literary labors during his lifetime, Pizarnik's fame has been mostly posthumous, achieving notoriety after her suicide. Contemporary literary critics have made her into an icon of feminist and, for some, lesbian poetics and the aesthetics of women's writing in Latin America. Her poetry reveals her own troubled existence (she suffered from clinical schizophrenia), her sensation of being forever an outsider and her sense of failure. She is often compared to the American poet Silvia Plath. Her poetry was highly regarded by Mexican Nobel laureate Octavio Paz, who wrote the preface to her 1962 collection of poems *Árbol de Diana* (Diana's tree). An intense focus on and preoccupation with the body are also evident in Pizarnik's writing.

One of her most fascinating, as well as disturbing, texts is her *La condesa sangrienta* (The bloody countess, 1971), a prose work based on the life of the sixteenth-century Hungarian countess Erzébet Bárthory, whom she discovered through a book written by the surrealist writer Valentine Penrose. Bárthory was infamous for torturing over 600 young maidens in sexual rituals intended to prolong her own youth. Contemporary criticism of this text has focused on its metaphoric value for interpreting the violent sociopolitical reality of Argentina, as well as relating its lesbian dimension to Pizarnik's own lesbian identity (Chávez-Silverman 1995).

MARTA LYNCH

Marta Lynch (1925–1985) stands out as one of the most notable contemporary Argentine women authors for her unabashed treatment of the ills that afflict the social body and her criticism of national myths. In spite of her prolific literary production and wide readership in Argentina, she remains one of the understudied figures of recent years and has yet to be translated into English. She is the author of both short stories and novels. Her fiction is well known for presenting a specifically feminist point of view and making no apologies about it. Her characters are generally middle-class women who are struggling to create their own identity and their own place within the male-dominated world. Her most memorable novels are *La señora Ordóñez* (Mrs. Ordóñez, 1967), *La penúltima versión de la Colorada Villanueva* (The penultimate version of Colorada Villanueva, 1978), and *Informe bajo llave* (Report under lock and key, 1983). A reading of these texts allows one to trace Lynch's commitment demonstrating the efficacy of literature as social commentary.

ENRIQUE MEDINA

One of the contemporary Argentine authors with the most mixed critical assessment is Enrique Medina (b. 1937), whose inaugural work is still considered one of his best: *Las tumbas* (The tombs, 1972). While many critics have denounced his work for his emphasis on the marginal, the scabrous, and the violent and other critics have accused his work of being a poor imitation of the prose style of yellow journalism, others have seen in his fictions and chronicles reliable interpretations of the underbelly of Argentine society. Medina's dirty realism focuses unrelentingly on social and cultural hypocrisies, with particular attention paid to class conflict, the oppression of women and other social subalterns, and the structural violence deriving from inherent features of an embedded authoritarianism in Argentine society. Medina's language is relentless in capturing not only the way people actually

Luisa Valenzuela. Courtesy of Editorial Sudamericana.

speak, but also in dissecting the double-speak of official discourse. While there is a documentary and a testimonial dimension to Medina's writings, especially the newspaper chronicles that have been his specialty in the last fifteen years, his writing also provides a sustained interpretive perspective on the pathetic drabness of the lives of most Argentines, despite all of the slogans of opportunity, prosperity, and sophistication.

LUISA VALENZUELA

More widely known outside of Argentina is Luisa Valenzuela (b. 1938) who, in fact, was better known in the United States than in Argentina until recently. Her works have been translated into English almost in their entirety, and she has earned an international reputation as a controversial Argentine writer. It is worth noting that she remained practically an unknown in Argentina until after the return to democracy in 1983, when her books began to be published in Buenos Aires. Her fiction (short stories and novels) addresses the recent political and social upheaval that has persisted in the country from the late 1960s through the 1980s.

Valenzuela's most well-known and one of her most politically motivated work is the 1983 *Cola de lagartija* (The lizard's tail). While the novel only thinly veils its treatment of real-life persons—the wizard is understood to be

Ricardo Piglia. Courtesy of Editorial Sudamericana.

José López Rega, the minister of welfare under the presidency of Isabel Perón—it is far from a realistic portrayal of events. Rather, it is a narrative that
relies heavily on fantasy and mythological realms of existence. Her more
recent *Novela negra con argentinos* (Black novel with Argentines, 1990) is
based loosely on the model of detective fiction. It deals with the subject of
exile, specifically a group of Argentine exiles living in New York City.

RICARDO PIGLIA

One of the most important authors to emerge in recent years is Ricardo
Piglia (b. 1941), who, although he began to write in the 1960s, was launched
to fame with his 1980 *Respiración artificial* (Artificial respiration). The novel
has come to represent the tremendous literary response to the violent military
repression that held the country captive between 1976 and 1983. Piglia's
work, like the many others written in response to the tyranny, speaks eloquently to the function of literature as a contestatory cultural vehicle of

expression. *Respiración artificial* is clearly the heir of such writers as Arlt and Borges, whose presence is virtually palpable in the text. The novel is patterned on the reconstruction of history that the protagonist, Emilio Renzi, must piece together. Renzi is the author of a novel based the life of his uncle, Marcelo Maggi. Piglia's novel opens with the fictional publication of the protagonist's novel in April 1976, just weeks after the military coup. The ensuing narration is the retelling of Renzi's efforts to locate his uncle and their subsequent mutual correspondence. Maggi, in turn, is doing research on a fictional nineteenth-century figure known as Enrique Ossorio. Ossorio was the supposed author of a novel titled *1979*, and Maggi shares with his nephew fragments of the novel that refer to episodes of violence, torture, and exile in Argentina's past. In this way, Piglia is able to contextualize the contemporary violence of the military without referring to it directly. This technique was very common among writers who remained in Argentina and who found it necessary to disguise the true subject of their writing with metaphor and allusion to past or fictional events. In this way they were able to avoid censorship and still write about the events taking place in the country.

LITERATURE IN THE 1990s

The 1990s has seen the emergence of a post-dictatorship generation of authors who are now more concerned with detailing the postmodern fragmentation of Argentine society initiated by the return to democracy and the encroaching multinational presence in the country as well as the worldwide globalization of culture. Many novels now seem to be informed by a sort of fin-de-siècle anxiety about the imminent arrival of a new millennium. A significant portion of the fiction being produced details futuristic, dystopian visions of a postnational society in decay. There has also been in recent years a resurgence of historical fiction. Authors seem to be responding to a public need or desire to reexamine the past. The lives of virtually every major historical figure from Sarmiento and Rosas to the Peróns have been fictionalized for public consumption, and historical novels are consistently at the top of the best-seller lists.

REFERENCES

Aizenberg, Edna. *The Aleph Weaver: Biblical, Kabbalistic and Judaic Elements in Borges.* Potomac, Md.: Scripta Humanistica, 1984.

Aizenberg, Edna, ed. *Borges and His Successors: The Borgesian Impact on Literature and the Arts.* Columbia: University of Missouri Press, 1990.

Balderston, Daniel. *Out of Context: Historical Reference and the Representation of Reality in Borges.* Durham, N.C.: Duke University Press, 1993.

Balderston, Daniel, et al. *Ficción y política: La narrativa argentina durante el proceso militar.* Buenos Aires: Alianza; Minneapolis: Institute for the Study of Ideologies and Literature, University of Minnesota, 1987.

Chávez Silverman, Suzanne. "The Look That Kills: The 'Unacceptable Beauty' of Alejandra Pizarnik's *La condesa sangrienta.*" *¿Entiendes? Queer Readings, Hispanic Writings.* Ed. Emilie L. Bergmann and Paul Julian Smith. Durham: Duke University Press, 1995. 281–305.

Colás, Santiago. *Postmodernity in Latin America: The Argentine Paradigm.* Durham, N.C.: Duke University Press, 1994.

Flori, Mónica R. *Streams of Silver: Six Contemporary Women Writers from Argentina.* Lewisburg: Bucknell University Press, 1995.

Foster, David William. *The Argentine Generation of 1880: Ideology and Cultural Texts.* Columbia: University of Missouri Press, 1990.

———. *Social Realism in the Argentine Narrative.* Chapel Hill: North Carolina Studies in the Romance Languages and Literatures, 1986.

———. *Violence in Argentine Literature: Cultural Responses to Tyranny.* Columbia: University of Missouri Press, 1995.

Goldberg, Florinda. *Alejandra Pizarnik: "Este espacio que somos."* Gaithersburg, Md.: Ediciones Hispamérica, 1994.

Goodrich, Diana Sorensen. *Facundo and the Construction of Argentine Culture.* Austin: University of Texas Press, 1996.

Kerr, Lucille. *Suspended Fictions: Reading the Novels of Manuel Puig.* Urbana: University of Illinois Press, 1987.

Kuhnheim, Jill S. *Gender, Politics, and Poetry in Twentieth-Century Argentina.* Gainesville: University Press of Florida, 1996.

Leland, Christopher Towne. *The Last Happy Men: The Generation of 1922, Fiction, and the Argentine Reality.* Syracuse, N.Y.: Syracuse University Press, 1986.

Lewis, Marvin A. *Afro-Argentine Discourse: Another Dimension of the Black Diaspora.* Columbia: University of Missouri Press, 1996.

Lichtblau, Myron I. *The Argentine Novel: An Annotated Bibliography.* Lanham, Md.: Scarecrow Press, 1997.

Lindstrom, Noami. *Jewish Issues in Argentine Literature: From Gerchunoff to Szichman.* Columbia: University of Missouri Press, 1989.

Ludmer, Josefina. *El género gauchesco: un tratado sobre la patria.* Buenos Aires: Sudamericana, 1988.

Masiello, Francine. *Between Civilization & Barbarism: Women, Nation, and Literary Culture in Modern Argentina.* Lincoln: University of Nebraska Press, 1992.

Peavler, Terry J. *Julio Cortázar*. New York: Twayne, 1990.

Piña, Cristina. *Alejandra Pizarnik*. Buenos Aires: Planeta, 1991.

Reati, Fernando. *Nombrar lo innombrable. Violencia política y novela argentina: 1975–1985*. Buenos Aires: Legasa, 1992.

Senkman, Leonardo. *La identidad judía en la literatura argentina*. Buenos Aires: Pardés, 1983.

Stavans, Ilán. *Julio Cortázar: A Study of the Short Fiction*. New York: Twayne, 1996.

Tittler, Jonathan. *Manuel Puig*. New York: Twayne, 1993.

7

Performing Arts

BUENOS AIRES is known throughout the Hispanic world as an important cosmopolitan cultural center. Visitors marvel at the city's sophistication, as seen in its exquisite opera house, the Colón, and in the street that never sleeps, Corrientes, the "Broadway of Buenos Aires." The theater is so vital in Buenos Aires that it has often been said that one can see a different production every night for an entire year and never repeat a performance. This chapter concerns some of the most important manifestations of the Argentine performing arts, most notably theater, music, and dance with special attention paid to that quintessential Argentine art—the tango.

THE TANGO

In popular imagination, tango is synonymous with Argentina, in spite of the fact that it is connected mainly to the capital city of Buenos Aires. The roots of the tango, which originated as a dance form in the end of the nineteenth century, can be traced to the port city bordellos where anxious immigrant men awaited their turns with the prostitutes by dancing with each other, locked in an embrace and engaging in intricate footwork. In turn-of-the-century Argentina there were many more men than women; in 1914, the gap was more than 100,000. Thus, brothels became popular throughout the city. Foreign women were routinely recruited to serve in the brothels, often with the complicity of the Buenos Aires police departments (Guy 1991, 63).

The tango represented a fusion of the music and dances of the many immigrant groups that lived in the port. The musical traditions of the immigrants from Southern Italy and Eastern Europe mingled with those from Southern Spain and Africa, who were already there.

The dance became popular with the lower classes and with it the art of the tango song emerged, connected to the *bandoneón* button accordion that was imported from Germany. The popular figure in the tango dance is the *compadre*, who may be seen as a sort of urban gaucho in the sense that he shared with his rural cousin a fierce masculinity and independence as well as a tendency to settle affairs of honor with a knife. All these elements became integral components of the early tango (Collier 1995, 37). This rough and tumble multicultural Buenos Aires was the world into which the dance was born.

The term itself is said to have either Portuguese or African roots. It most probably arrived via the slave trade. Throughout the Hispanic world, the tango became known as a site where African slaves would gather to dance (Collier 1995, 41). Later, the word became associated with black dances in general. The influence of *candomble*, a popular dance based on a religion brought to the new world by African slaves that involves frenzied dancing in an effort to induce an individual into a trance-like state, may be observed in the complicated steps of the tango, although it was not danced in an embrace, but rather with the couple separated (1995, 43). It was the *compadritos*, the immigrant ruffians who lived in the ports, who first took the dance the Africans called the tango and, trying to mock its movements, incorporated it into the *milonga*, a couple's dance that had its origins in the *habanera*, imported, as this name implies, from Cuba. The *habanera*, in turn, had its roots in the Spanish *contradanza* (45).

In all probability, this new way of dancing the *milonga* actually fostered the creation of the tango. Although the dance created a scandal in Buenos Aires polite society, it was introduced to Europe at the beginning of the century and became popular. In 1911 the new dance reached Paris and created quite a stir. Then, as now, success in Paris was considered the ultimate Argentine aspiration—the official seal of cultural approval. Thus, the dance became ever more popular in Buenos Aires and no longer only among the poor immigrant class but among the wealthy as well. It was after World War I that the tango achieved its international notoriety—inseparable from the voice of the greatest Argentine tango singer who ever lived, Carlos Gardel.

Charles Romuald Gardès, who later became known as Carlos Gardel, was born in France in 1890 but came to Buenos Aires in 1893. His father had been a married businessman, and his father's lover, Gardel's mother Doña Berta, brought the boy to the country and ironed clothes to support her family. While Gardel was growing up he engaged in odd jobs and attended the theater whenever possible. There were two principal influences in Gardel's life: the opera singers at the theaters he used to frequent and the *payadores*, or folksingers, who improvised their songs to their own guitar accompaniment. Although Gardel never was a *payador*, he learned the many folk songs they sang, and he became well known in the poorer barrios of Buenos Aires as a folksinger. Gardel met José Razzano (1887–1960) in 1911 and the two became singing partners in what would become a very popular partnership that lasted until 1925.

The singers recorded more than 100 folk songs together and performed throughout the city in cabarets, cinemas, theaters, and on the radio. In 1917 Victor Records recorded Gardel's first tango, "Mi noche triste" (My sad night) (Evans "The Sultry Tango," 1988, 119). After that, Gardel met with success after success. When Razzano started to suffer from a throat condition, Gardel began to record alone, and he made more than 900 recordings by himself (Azzi 1995, 124). He began to gain fame in Europe and starred in seven films, all with Paramount Studios, three in France and four in the United States. In 1932 lyricist Alfredo Le Pera, who wrote Gardel's scripts and the songs for his films, joined Gardel. Gardel's voice was so popular that occasionally the audience would demand that the projectionist rewind the film in order to hear yet again one of his tangos. It was in 1935, at the zenith of his career, while the singer was on a tour of Puerto Rico, Caracas, Maracaibo, Barranquilla, Cartagena, and Bogotá, that he died. On June 24, in Medellín, Colombia, the plane he and Le Pera were in collided with another on the airfield, killing them both. Gardel's body arrived in Buenos Aires in February 1936, and thousands of fans followed the hearse to the Chacaritas cemetery.

The cultlike following that the man, Argentina's first international star, engendered is still present today. Argentines say that Gardel sings better all the time. Gardel's voice and tremendous charisma made him successful not only in Argentina but throughout the Hispanic world. As in the case of Eva Perón, a death at the height of one's career is a ticket to immortality. Photos of the icon are seen everywhere in Buenos Aires, and his voice can still be heard on scratchy recordings from the 1920s and 1930s. Gardel's tomb in the Chacarita cemetery has a larger than life statue of the idol, and to this day one can often see a lit cigarette in his hand, a continuing tribute left by his fans, much the way a votive candle might be kept next to a religious icon. In fact, in many Argentine homes, one can see the smiling face of Gardel placed next to pictures of saints.

The popularity of the tango went into a decline but then resurfaced in the

1940s when General Juan Perón decreed that all radio stations play Argentine music at least 50 percent of the time. While that decree helped evoke a renewed interest in the tango, it damaged another part of the Peronist plan, which was to purify the Spanish language by banning *lunfardo*, the slang so common in tango lyrics. This odd form of censorship was enforced until 1949.

The greatest tango musicians, including Astor Piazzolla and Osvaldo Pugliese, are known throughout the world. It is interesting to note that the first tango musicians were of African-Argentine origins. At the turn of the century, talented musicians from Buenos Aires began to participate in the tango bands, and the music developed in its own right, with the most important element being the *bandoneón*. Tango trios began to play on city streets and in cafés, and the music itself, as opposed to the dance, became the focus of attention (Collier 1995, 57).

The instruments central to the tango orchestra are the *bandoneón*, violin, piano, and double bass. In the 1920s the tango musicians split into two groups, the "evolutionists" and the "traditionalists." The evolutionists, devoted to the development and refinement of the tango, worked toward a music that would ultimately have depth and complexity. The evolutionist groups generally included two *bandoneóns*, two violins, a double bass, and piano. The traditionalists, on the other hand, stressed rhythm and the need to develop a more danceable tango. The traditionalist groups had three or four *bandoneóns* and three or four violins. Traditionalists later brought in clarinets, drums, and even trumpets (Azzi 1995, 120).

The *bandoneón* player Aníbal Carmelo Troilo (1914–1975), known as "Pucho, el Gordo," or the fat man, is second only to Carlos Gardel is terms of the tango elite in Argentine history. He formed his own tango group in 1937 and played at the Tibidabo cabaret for sixteen years. He is considered to be the greatest *bandoneón* player of all time. The entire country—most especially the city of Buenos Aires—mourned his death in 1975. In fact, the day of Pucho's birth is still celebrated every July 11 as *Bandoneón* Day. December 11, the birthday of Gardel, is celebrated as National Tango Day.

At the turn of the century, tango musicians were becoming celebrities, as were some of the singers and dancers. The earliest, and some consider greatest, tango dance star was Ovidio Bianquet (1879–1942) known as "El Cachafaz" (Barefaced Cheek), or Cacha. When he beat out a popular contestant in a tango dance contest in 1915 his future was assured, and from then on he was given free access to all the dance halls in the city. He has always been regarded as the greatest dancer of all. He died in a dance salon just as he was getting up to dance another tango with his longtime partner, Carmencita Calderón.

In the 1910s tango became an international sensation. It was the rage in France, Britain, Italy, Spain, and Russia. When the Argentine ambassador to Russia was introduced to Tsar Nicolas, his response was reported to be, "Argentina, ah yes! The tango!" (Cooper 1995, 96). It was said that Spain's Alfonso XIII loved the tango, although some of his royal entourage were scandalized by the dance. The dance took New York by storm in 1913 and 1914. The Catholic Church in New York became the first religious organization officially to deem the tango immoral. The city's cardinal in 1913 recalled 600 invitations to a dance in which it was thought that the tango might be seen; the entire city was thus warned of the cardinal's personal opposition to the dance (1995, 93).

It is interesting to note that the tango has maintained a following in two unlikely places: Finland and Japan. Oddly enough, the dance enjoyed such popularity in Finland that it became the Finnish national dance, and it is no longer associated with the Southern Cone country where it originated. The only great distinction between the Argentine tango and its Finnish cousin lies in where it is seen and performed. In Finland the dance is connected to the countryside, not the urban centers. Japan became one of the primary cultural centers of tango during the early part of this century, and Japanese tango bands were formed in the 1930s, 1940s, and 1950s. It was not until 1964, however, that Argentines actually played a tango concert in Japan, although many followed in subsequent years.

The golden age of tango was said to occur from roughly 1920 until the early 1940s. During this time the dance enjoyed an unprecedented popularity throughout all levels of Argentine society. People listened to tango musical groups, sang their favorite songs, watched their favorite tango performers on film, and, of course, danced the tango. Many *tangueros*, or tango dancers, followed their favorite bands around the city. One of the most famous tango centers was the National café on Corrientes Street, known as the "Cathedral of Tango" (Azzi 1995, 115). On its opening night, an all-women's orchestra played, and the locale continued to be a mainstay in tango nightlife for almost four decades. Although women's tango bands were quite common in the 1920s and 1930s, none of them ever made recordings.

There were also many female tango singers, many of whom dressed as men, such as Azucena Maizani (1902–1970). Maizani, who started her career in 1920, was promptly given the nickname "Azabache" (jet black) because of her black hair. Later she was given yet another, "La Ñata Gaucha" (the snub-nosed gaucha). When she premiered the tango "Padre nuestro" in the National Theater in 1923, she was called back for five encores (Azzi 1995, 141). Some women, such as María Luisa Carnelli (1898–1987), also wrote tango lyrics. Carnelli was one of the most prolific tango lyricists of the day; however, she wrote most of her songs under a male pseudonym, either Luis Mario or Mario Castro, in order to keep her gender hidden.

Eventually women became more accepted as lyricists and singers, and they did not have to cross-dress or change their names. The fame of La Ñata was followed by that of other female tango singers, including Libertad Lamarque, Mercedes Simone, and Tita Merello, all of whom recorded in the 1930s and also starred in movies.

Jorge Luis Borges once said that the tango lyric would go down in Argentine history as the true poetry of its time (Azzi 1995, 132). To be sure, the tango songs were poetry, and they generally revealed the sadness and melancholy in the life of the *compadrito*. The songs refer to his idolization of his mother, fatalism, and nostalgia for his childhood neighborhood that has changed and become virtually unrecognizable. The protagonist is tormented by his failures in love and life. The lyrics of the tango are often said to represent the soul of Buenos Aires.

Many tango lyrics refer to the poor Milonguita, a woman paid to dance the tango with clients. She is the tango version of the classic Latin American soap-opera protagonist, the poor girl from the wrong side of the tracks who dreams of becoming rich and famous. The tango was still often associated with prostitution, and the recipe for making the most money for many women was to be a skilled dancer. The dance was simply considered the prelude to sex, and three tangos were generally enough to heat things up (Azzi 1995, 118).

In the 1950s the tango was on the decline, but in the 1960s a new sort of tango, represented by avant-garde musician Astor Piazzolla (1921–1992), developed. Piazzolla was born in Argentina, but he grew up in New York City where he even played a bit role as a newspaper seller in the classic Gardel film *El día que me quieras* (The day you love me, 1935) (Azzi 1995, 157). Piazzolla returned to Argentina, moved to the capital, and began to play in various groups, which culminated in the formation of his Quinteto Nuevo Tango in 1960 with a *bandoneón*, piano, violin, guitar, and double bass. He introduced dissonance, chromatic harmony, and a wider range of rhythm to the tango, creating a sound that was difficult for most purists to accept and for most musicians to play. Piazzolla composed more than 750 works, including concertos and film and theatrical scores. In the 1970s and 1980s he became famous internationally for his unique take on tango, and his influence can be heard in much tango music today.

Although the dance suffered a decline in the 1950s, 1960s, and 1970s, it again rebounded with a vengeance with the popularity of a number of movies and shows in which it was highlighted during the 1980s and 1990s. The musical production of *Tango Argentino*, which opened in 1983 in Paris, told the history of the dance. It played to sold-out audiences around the United States and Europe throughout much of the 1980s. *Tango X 2*, a tribute to Gardel, played to sold-out crowds in Latin America, Eastern and Western Europe, and the Far East in 1988. The Hollywood movie starring Madonna and based on the life of Argentina's first lady Eva Perón, *Evita* (1995), included many scenes with the pop goddess locked in the passionate dance. Tango also had a featured role in a film starring a tangoing Al Pacino, *Scent of a Woman* (1992), as well as a 1994 movie starring Arnold Schwarzenegger, *True Lies*. In fact, partly as a result of this renewed international interest, the National Academy of Tango was founded in 1990 in the heart of Buenos Aires on Avenida de Mayo.

While the tango remains Argentina's foremost contribution to the world in terms of dance and music, there is a significant body of folk music and folk dances in the country. The dances of the various regions of Argentina show a marked influence of their neighboring countries. The *zamba* is a dance in which the partners use a handkerchief, much like the famous *cueca* of Chile, and engage in a flirtatious exchange. In the Cuyo region, along the border with Chile in the provinces of San Juan, Mendoza, and San Luis, the *tonada*, the *gato*, and the *cueca* are common and are danced by a non-embracing couple. Generally, the main instrument is the guitar. The *requinto cuyo*, a variation of the guitar with more strings, originated in this region. The lyrics are generally about love, although historical and religious subjects are also common.

In the regions that border Paraguay, such as Misiones and Corrientes, the *polca* and the *galopa* are danced, and the indigenous Gauraní influences are apparent. The harp, probably the most popular Paraguayan instrument, is often used. In the region that borders Uruguay, the *chamarrita* can be heard, which is similar to the *sobre-paso* of Uruguay. The *chamamé*, with variations that may be heard throughout Santa Fe and Santiago del Estero, has a melodious, sometimes rhythmic sound. In Santiago del Estero, traditional rhythms like the *chacarera*, the *gato*, and the *escondido* may be heard, performed by soloists, duets, or bands using guitars or the *bombo legüero*, a percussion instrument that originated in that city. In Salavina, a region of the country where Quechua is spoken, the songs are bilingual. In the southern part of the Córdoba province, Tulumba, the *chacarera* is characteristic as are the *zamba*, the *jota cordobesa*, the *bailecito cordobés*, and the *gato*. In Tucumán the *zamba* is thought of as the national dance. Salta, in the north of Argentina, is the home of the *zamba* as well, and in the Jujuy province the influence of Bolivia is felt throughout all of the folk music through the use of the pan flute and other instruments common to that area.

In Patagonia, in the southern end of Argentina, the singing and music are greatly influenced by the indigenous communities that inhabit the region. The dances, such as the *loncomeo*, the *cordillerana*, the *chorrillero*, and the *kaani*, have little choreography and are performed to such traditional instruments as the *kultrán* (percussion), a sort of box that is rhythmically hit with a stick.

The *payadores* emerged in La Pampa as well as in the southern Santa Fe region and southern Entre Ríos region. The *payadores* render songs on the spot, often with a rival singing the counterpoint. Their improvisations are sung to the chords of the *milonga*, the *cifra*, the *triunfo*, or even the waltz. There is also a musician, known as the *criollo* reciter, who recites poetry concerned with depicting manners. This all forms part of the River Plate folklore, and it has a similar dissemination in Uruguay. More than 100 traditional and original dances can be traced to this region, all of which are danced by a non-embracing couple.

In the 1950s and 1960s Argentine folk music experienced a great revival, and many of the groups remain popular today, including Los Chalchaleros and Los Fronterizos. Eduardo Falú remains one of the country's most beloved folksingers, as does Mercedes Sosa from Tucumán, a folksinger also known for her strong political protests during the dictatorship of 1976–1983.

The study of Argentine folklore, information regarding the myths, popular language, clothing, medicine, songs, and proverbs, began in the second half of the nineteenth century when Ventura R. Lynch (1851–1883) published a pamphlet about the songs, dances, poetry, and stories of the gaucho. The pamphlet was reedited in 1953 by A. R. Cortazar as *Folklore bonarense*. Another Argentine scholar who contributed to the interest in the country's folklore was Samuel LaFone Quevedo who studied the ruins and myths of the indigenous population of the northeast.

Juan Bautista Ambrosetti (1865–1917) published in 1893 the first work that initiated the science of folklore with his text *Materiales para el estudio del folklore* which concentrated on his work in the northeast. In 1921 the Consejo Nacional de Educación (National Council on Education), concerned with Argentine folklore, initiated a massive study on the topic. Juan

Alfonso Carrizo (1895–1957) gathered over 20,000 songs from throughout the northeast and was able to trace the Spanish heritage that operated in popular poetry, which he published in *Antecedentes hispanomedievales de la poesia tradicional argentina,* in 1945. Usmael Mpya (1900–1981) was the first systematically to study the *payadores,* or poetic duels in Córdoba, La Rioja, and Santiago del Estero in his *El arte de los payadores* (1959). In 1960 Buenos Aires hosted the International Folklore Festival with delegates converging in the city from around the world.

While tango may be said to be the emblematic music of Argentina and folk music plays a prominent place in the development of the musical history of the country, what must not be overlooked is the development of the Argentine opera and classical music. To give an indication of the level of importance accorded to high culture in Argentina during the mid-nineteenth century one need know only that, in 1854, thirty operas were produced in the city.

MUSIC

During the second half of the nineteenth century, many musical societies were formed in Buenos Aires which organized instrumental and symphonic concerts. The Philharmonic Society formed in 1852 and lasted until 1859. The German immigrant population aided in the diffusion of classical music and formed choral groups, such as the Sociedad Alemana de Canto (German Song Society) in 1862 and the Concordia group in 1863. By 1865 nine musical societies had been formed, and by the end of the century foreign artists were regularly coming to Buenos Aires to perform.

The year 1877 marked the first concert in which Argentine instrumentalists played the music of Mozart, Beethoven, Brahms, and Saint-Saens. The first institution devoted to the study of music was the Escuela de Música del Estado (School of the Music of the State) founded in 1867. Another was formed in 1875 and eventually conservatories became common throughout the city.

Francisco Hargreaves (1849–1900) may be considered one of the most important figures in the development of a distinctly Argentine opera. He studied in Italy but returned to Argentina and used his native country's themes as an inspiration in his work. His first opera, *La gata blanca* (The white cat) was presented in Italy in 1876 and in Buenos Aires in 1877. His second, *El vampiro* (The vampire), an opera in three acts, won an honorary mention in a competition in Milan in 1881.

It was in 1874 that a series of Conciertos Nacionales, or National Concerts, began to be held in the city; in these concerts, native-born composers and musicians could demonstrate their talents. Also in this year the city was treated to the first concert given by an Argentine pianist, Amancio Alcorta, playing his own music. In 1880 Juan Gutiérrez founded the National Conservatory of Music, and in 1893 Alberto Williams (1862–1952) founded the Buenos Aires Music Conservatory. Opera became so important in Buenos Aires that the latest European operas routinely opened in the city only months after their European debut.

Williams was a very important figure in Argentine music history. A pianist and composer, he studied in Paris and returned to Buenos Aires in 1889. He wrote nine symphonies on national themes and devoted his life to the instruction of young musicians. In 1897 three operas written by Argentines were staged in Buenos Aires, including *La pampa*, written by Arturo Berutti about the gaucho Juan Moreira. Although it was written in Italian, rural Argentina inspired the music and scenery.

From 1880 to 1910, the evolution of music in Buenos Aires accelerated as a result of the large groups of immigrants arriving in the city. In 1924 El Ateneo was formed to bring together writers and artists under the direction of poet Carlos Guido y Spano. The organization, dedicated to the promulgation of the arts in Buenos Aires, was divided into three branches: literature, music, and fine arts. In October 1925 the Ateneo put on its first symphonic concert in the Teatro Opera, featuring the music of Wagner and conducted by Alberto Williams. Many famous soloists from around the world converged on Buenos Aires, and the result was a fertilization of national talent. Argentines began to travel to Europe to study as well, mostly in France, Spain, and Italy, and returned to their native country where they assimilated the new information into national themes connected principally to gaucho folklore and indigenous populations.

Two main strands developed in the evolution of national music at the turn of the century: music related to the indigenous dimension and music related to the expression of life in Buenos Aires. In 1925 another strand was added, that of the universalists, who believed in combining all elements, national and international, rural and urban, to develop their own unique sound.

THE OPERA

Some of the most important national operas to debut include *Tucumán* (music by Felipe Boero; lyrics by Leopoldo Díaz) in 1918, the first opera not only written by an Argentine but also played and directed by Argentines. Another important opera, *Lázaro* by Constantino Gaito with lyrics by Víctor Mercante, premiered in 1929. This opera is notable because it takes place in the province of Buenos Aires and incorporated, for the first time, the tango in a musical production for the enjoyment of the high society. Another opera by Gaito, *La sangre de las guitarras* (The blood of the guitars), premiered in 1932 and received outstanding reviews, as much for the music as for the elegant staging and costumes that were meant to depict the period of Rosas. This was considered to be a culminating moment in national opera history. In the 1940s and 1950s other Argentine operas were produced, and in the 1950s two musical productions based on the plays of Federico García-Lorca were presented with critical success, *Bodas de sangre* (Blood wedding) and *La zapatera prodigiosa* (The prodigious shoemaker woman).

SYMPHONY

In the development of the symphony, Alfredo Schiuma met with critical success with his *La pampa*. Later, tango became incorporated into Argentine symphony in the works of Juan José Castro, Jacobo Ficher, Emilio Napolitano, and Juan Francisco Giacobbe. During the 1940s Argentine Héctor Panizza became the first director of the Metropolitan Opera in New York.

Formal musical associations have a long and important history in Argentina, beginning in 1894 when, in Buenos Aires, the Sociedad Musical de Mutua Protección (Buenos Aires Musical Society of Mutual Protection), a musical union of sorts, was formed. This group changed its name and became the Asociación del Profesorado Orquestral (Association of Orchestral Professors) and enjoyed its best years from 1922 to 1930. In the 1920s European opera groups spent their off-seasons in Buenos Aires. In 1924 the Orchestra of the Colón stopped relying on musicians imported from Europe for each season and became solidly the domain of national musicians. Other important symphonic organizations formed include the Orquesta Sinfónica de la Ciudad de Buenos Aires (Symphonic Orchestra of Buenos Aires), founded in 1949, which would later become known as the Philharmonic. In 1949 the Orquesta Sinfónica del Estado (Symphonic Orchestra of the State), later known as the National Symphony, was formed. Finally, in 1951, the Orquestra Sinfónica de Radio del Estado (Symphonic Orchestra of State Radio), which later became the Radio Nacional—was established by Bruno Bandini and began to offer free concerts in the Faculty of Law and Social Sciences at the university.

THE COLÓN OPERA HOUSE

It is impossible to discuss the performing arts in Argentina without mentioning one of the most well-known buildings in the world, the Colón Opera

House, home to both the National Symphony Orchestra and the National Ballet. The Colón, built at the turn of the century, represents the epitome of Buenos Aires's high culture. The building, designed by Italian architect Francisco Tamburini, took eighteen years to complete (Perrottet 1988, 125). Mikhail Baryshnikov, the Russian ballet star, called the Colón, "The most beautiful of all of the theaters I know" (Perrottet 1988, 124). The performance hall itself is enough to take away one's breath. The Colón seats 2,437 and has space for 4,000 more to stand. A domed ceiling features a mural by Raúl Soldi done in the 1960s. The mural, which has fifty-one figures, are all connected in some way with music. From the ceiling of the Colón hangs one of the largest chandeliers in the world with over 600 lightbulbs.

Actually, this is the second Colón theatre in the history of the city. The first Colón, which opened in 1857, seated 2,000 spectators and was located on the Plaza de Mayo where the Banco de la Nación sits today. It was at the original Colón that Argentines first developed a taste for opera and the symphony. The very first performance held at the original Colón was Giuseppe Verdi's *La Traviata* presented by an Italian company. The theater served for many years not only as an opera house but also as a site for ballet, poetic and literary conferences, and even civic meetings. In 1888 the building was sold to the Banco de la Nación and in 1944 it was demolished.

The architecture of the new Colón is a combination of nineteenth-century German-Italian Renaissance and French classical styles. Verdi's *Aida* was the first opera presented in the new Colón, on May 25, 1908. Before the opera began, the orchestra, under the direction of Luis Mancinelli, played the Argentine national anthem in an exquisite building many have called acoustically perfect. The crowd was so enthusiastic that it demanded the anthem be played again. In its inaugural year, the new Colón also included in its repertoire an opera in three acts written by Argentine Héctor Panizza entitled *Aurora*. This opera had as its setting the city of Córdoba during the time of the revolution and concerned the struggle for independence.

The Colón has presented Argentines with internationally known orchestras, operas, and ballet companies. Beneath the Colón theater's main stage there are three floors of workshop areas and rooms to store costumes and construct backdrops. There are 30,000 pairs of shoes alone stored at the Colón. Under the theater there is a rehearsal room with the same dimensions as the main stage upstairs to allow performers to practice while another event is being staged (Perrottet 1988, 125).

DANCE

The history of Argentine ballet unfolded on the stage of the Colón. The history of dance, among other things, in Argentina may be traced to the classical Spanish dance schools that emerged in Buenos Aires in the mid-nineteenth century. It was in the first part of that century that early professional and academic dance emerged. The year 1867 saw the first choreographed performances of ballet in Buenos Aires, held at the old Colón. The Rousset Company presented the great romantic ballets, such as *Giselle*, composed by Adolphe Adam (1803–1856). It was in the old Colón that a number of the most important international dance figures were able to present their ballets. In 1860 and 1861 the Thierry Company, the most important group to arrive in Buenos Aires, had a number of successes.

With the opening of the new Colón in 1908 ballet continued to be produced, and between the years 1913 and 1917 Argentina was first introduced to the art of modern ballet. The new Colón is the seat of Argentine ballet. Although many foreign-born dancers had appeared at the Colón, in 1925 the Cuerpo de Baile del Teatro Colón (Dance Company of the Colón Theater) presented their first performance, *The Golden Rooster* by Nikolay Rimsky-Korsakov. This Colón group is the oldest ballet organization in South America. Some of the dancers, including María Ruanova and Lide Martinoli, became internationally known. Margarita Wallman took over the choreographic leadership at the end of the 1930s and stayed until the end of the 1940s. She developed the ballet on a grand scale. Foreign dance groups continued to appear at the Colón as well. Throughout the 1950s Argentine ballet dancers continued to develop and present their talents in the Colón, and other internationally known performers performed in Buenos Aires. In the 1960s the Colón began to present the great ballet productions with internationally known dancers, such as Rudolf Nureyev, the well-known Russian star.

On October 10, 1971, Argentine ballet suffered a cruel blow when ten members of the ballet group from the Colón lost their lives in a plane crash in the Río de la Plata. They had been on their way to the city of Trelew, where they were scheduled to make an appearance. The news of the crash stunned the country. Argentine's most promising dancers had lost their lives, and it remains one of the saddest chapters in the history of Argentine dance.

In the 1980s two Argentine stars became international sensations—Julio Bocca and Maximiliano Guerra. Guerra, in 1987, received a silver medal in an international competition held in New York City and received a gold medal in another international competition in Varna, Bulgaria. He joined the English National Ballet as a principal dancer and performed in Buenos Aires in 1989 with that company in Pyotr Ilich Tchaikovsky's *Lago de los cisnes* (*Swan Lake*) in the Colón.

Julio Bocca, who was born in Argentina in 1967, studied dance at the Colón. Before finishing his studies he was named the Primer Bailarín by the Teresa Carreno Foundation of Venezuela and by the Municipal Theater in Rio de Janeiro. In 1985, in an international competition held in Moscow, he received the gold medal and, in 1987, he signed with the American Ballet Theater in New York, where he still dances today. He has performed as a visiting artist in a number of prestigious ballet companies around the world, including the Royal Ballet of London, the Bolshoi of Moscow, and La Scala of Milan, and has starred in ballets choreographed especially for him. In 1990 he founded the Ballet Argentino, a group dedicated to the promotion and training of young Argentines in dance.

THEATER

Another well-known theater in Buenos Aires is the Teatro Nacional Cervantes, located a few blocks from the Colón and inaugurated in 1921. The Cervantes was made as a monument to Spain to highlight Argentina's connection to Spain as well as to serve as the home of the national Argentine theater company. The front of the building is a copy of the front of the university in the Spanish city of Alcalá de Henares, done in the same Renaissance style (Urquiza 1968, 31). The luxurious interior, including such elements as mirrors and detailed tiles and tapestries from many cities in Spain, makes it a theater truly emblematic of the entire country of Spain. In the central theater there is room for 1,350 spectators. Don Alfonso XIII of Spain was so exited about the project that he insisted that any boat leaving from Spain for Argentina carry art objects to be used in the construction of the Cervantes (1968, 37). A fire, however, destroyed much of the original detail of the inside of the theater in 1961. In 1968, after extensive remodeling, the theater reopened and it continues to play an important role in the theatrical life of the city.

Theater in Argentina, like opera and the symphony, has always been considered of utmost importance. It was none other than the country's greatest national hero, José de San Martín, who said that a theater is a moral and political establishment of great authority (Fernández 1992, 14). It was only nine years after the May Revolution in 1810 that Argentina saw its first theatrical hit with *El hipócrita político*, a play adapted from Molière's *Tartuffe*.

In spite of this early interest, national theater is usually said to have originated in the circus in the year 1886 amid the puppet shows, acrobatics, and clown antics. It was in the circus that theater began to flourish when the Uruguayan Podestá brothers put on a pantomime production of *Juan Moreira*, the novel by Eduardo Gutiérrez. The play concerns a gaucho's attempts to cope with the rapidly changing world around him. It was thought that his sense of dislocation and frustration was shared by many in the country at that time and may have accounted for the play's enormous success. The first time the play was presented, on June 2, 1884, it was accompanied by music. Two years later, in a subsequent production, it was decided that the actor would use his own voice.

What is of great interest is how the pantomime of *Juan Moreira* itself evolved. To the central story of the gaucho other scenes were added, including regional song and dance, *payadas* (poetic duels by gauchos) and card games, as well as other customs, all of which added to the popular flavor of the show. Among the additions was the popular figure of humorous Cocoliche, the Creolized Italian who spoke in a Neapolitan-accented Spanish.

It was in these early productions of *Juan Moreira* that members of the public were even invited to participate in the play in minor roles (Pellarolo 1997, 90). Changes would even be made in the representation depending on the demographics of the given locale (Pellettieri 1990, 18). Thus, what began as a rural drama became transformed into a modern, urban play in which the immigrant contributions to national life were also presented.

After *Juan Moreira*, theater began to take on a decidedly national flavor. Theaters no longer provided the Argentine population merely with Italian, French, British, or American plays. By the end of the nineteenth century, theater was not only the domain of the circus; Buenos Aires had luxurious theaters that rivaled those of Europe where the wealthy could enjoy shows (Fernández 1992, 15). At the same time, however, Argentina experienced a tremendous wave of immigrants who arrived with little money. The circus continued to offer them a diversion.

Zarzuelas (musical comedies), *sainetes* (farces), and other popular forms originating in Spain are referred to as the *género chico criollo* that began to flourish in Buenos Aires at this time. The *sainete* delighted the audience through caricatures and social satire. The *sainete criollo* was the adaptation of the *sainete* to the specific Argentine context. The plays were tragicomedies that dealt with the difficulties of immigrant life. While the popular theater of the *sainete criollo* saw the fruitless struggles of the immigrants as a cause for laughter, it also served, as Silvia Pellarolo has pointed out, as a forum in which the subaltern immigrant community could reflect on their daily lives as part of the multicultural milieu that was forming an Argentine national identity at the turn of the century (1997, 217).

The *grotesco criollo* depicted the dehumanization of the immigrant experience: the immigrants' sense of dislocation in the new country and their inability to escape their miserable lot in life. The central topic for the *grotesco criollo* revolved around the vanquished dreams of the new immigrant when faced with the harsh realities of the New World.

Florencio Sánchez, who was born in Uruguay in 1875 and died in Italy in 1910, is considered the first national dramatist of great importance in Argentina and, in general, in Latin America as a whole. Argentines feel that it was a mere accident of birth that Sánchez was, in fact, Uruguayan. The controversy continues as to which country can claim him as their native son. Sánchez lived in Argentina for many years, and his plays were staged in Argentina. His two most important plays were *Barranca abajo*, a rural tragedy about an elderly man who loses everything he owns, and *La gringa*, which featured the conflict between an old gaucho and an Italian immigrant.

Unfortunately, after Sánchez, there was a decline in national theater that lasted for four decades, beginning with the coup d'état of General José Félix Uriburu in 1930. The fervor for the theater was reduced drastically, evidenced by the fact that in 1910 the average number of theatrical productions seen per year was 2.6 and by 1980 this number was a mere 0.2 per year (Fernández 1992, 17). Although theater languished for a period of time, three playwrights reached a degree of importance: Francisco Defilippis Novoa (1890–1930), a practitioner of grotesque theater; Samuel Eichelbaum (1894–1967), known for his introspective dramas that emphasize moral or spiritual crises; and Armando Discépolo (1887–1971), probably considered the greatest of the three, who founded of the *grotesco criollo*. Discépolo's plays, influential from 1910 to 1950, dealt with Italian immigrants and their conflicts with their Argentine-born children. The author himself was known to view his own theatrical endeavors as a way in which to arrive at the comic by way of the dramatic and fatalistic.

European authors such as Luigi Pirandello and theorists such as Erwin Piscator and Konstantin Stanislavski had a significant impact on Argentine theater in the early part of this century (Fernández 1992, 19). During the same year that Uriburu took power, 1930, Leónidas Barletta founded the Teatro del Pueblo (People's theater) and the independent Argentine theater finally emerged. The Teatro del Pueblo, which had a strong sociopolitical commitment, sought to develop a new public that would be more critically sophisticated. It was during this time that Argentina produced its first truly great national playwright, Roberto Arlt. Arlt's theater, like his fiction, dealt with the fantastic and the ambiguous, and his dreamlike focus was on the humiliations and resentments of the poor.

By the mid-1940s, Argentina entered into another period of theatrical spectacle, only this time the lavish productions were staged for the masses in the Plaza de Mayo and starred Juan and Eva Perón. During the Peronist stage of Argentine history, there was a focus on the members of the poorer classes, and artists and intellectuals were regarded with suspicion. It should therefore not come as any great surprise that little of depth and significance was produced in the cultural arena during those years. The theater remained independent; however, the plays that were produced were in accordance with the official ideology of Peronism. The production of Carlos Gorostiza's *El puente* is an exception. The play, the first great success of an Argentine author in the independent theater, dealt, like all of Gorostiza's plays, with the need for individuals to confront the truth and not give in to the tyranny of indifference.

The five dramatists that formed the most important theatrical group in Buenos Aires in the 1950s were Gorostiza (b. 1920), Osvaldo Dragún (b. 1929), Agustín Cuzzani (1924–87), Andrés Lizarraga (1919–82) and Juan Carlos Gené (b. 1928). These authors became well known during the cultural opening that followed the fall of Perón in 1955. There was a brief moment of optimism after the departure of Perón, but the illusions of a true democracy were thwarted and the country entered into a period of ferocious repression. These were the formative years of what would become the Generation of 1960.

The theater in the Generation of 1960 was characterized by profound disenchantment. During this time, the national theater was beginning to give way to smaller groups, theater workshops in which actors, playwrights, directors, and others gathered and developed a new system of interpretive work that was collaborative in nature. It was one of these groups, the Teatro de la Máscara, that premiered what could be considered the most important work of the Generation of 1960, *Soledad para cuatro* (Loneliness for four; 1961), written by Ricardo Halac in conjunction with director Augusto Fernández and the actors who presented it. The actors were working under the Stanislovskian method, with an emphasis on a profound and visceral identification with the personage they were representing. The playwrights of the 1960s wanted to present their frustration with the political, economic, and social reality of their country. Their theater did not focus on solutions to these problems as much as on the need to raise the consciousness of the audience to stark reality. The playwrights used a realistic theatrical mode along the lines of Arthur Miller's *Death of a Salesman*. Ten authors formed the core of the Generation of 1960: Halac (b. 1935), Sergio De Cecco (1931–1986), Ricardo Talesnik (b. 1935), Julio Mauricio (b. 1919), Carlos Somigliana (1932–1987), Oscar Viale (1932–94), Germán Rozenmacher (1936–1971), Roberto Cossa (b. 1934), Griselda Gambaro (b. 1928), and Eduardo Pavlovsky (b. 1933). The last two are included in the Generation of 1960 although they did not write plays that were realistic in any way during that decade.

Toward the end of the 1960s and the beginning of the 1970s Argentina underwent a series of dramatic sociopolitical changes. In 1966 General Juan Carlos Onganía headed a military coup, and the country entered into a period of dictatorship. A guerrilla movement formed and played an important part in Argentine history through the 1970s. It was a period of generalized violence that caused writers to become more politicized. They presented plays about what was happening in the country and what could happen if things continued status quo.

Theater of cruelty, based on the ideas of Antonin Artaud, was used to make a statement about the sociopolitical reality of the country, and it became a common format for dramatists. *El avión negro*, a play presented in 1970 and written by four of the most important dramatists of the Generation of 1960, Cossa, Rozenmacher, Somigliana, and Talesnik, concerns the imagined return to Argentina of exiled leader Juan Perón. New theater groups from the left were also beginning to make a mark in the country, including the Teatro Payró, the Teatro del Centro, and the Teatro Popular de la Ciudad—all of which included very politically charged plays in their repertoires. Many new important dramatists appeared, among them Aída Bortnik (b. 1942), Diana Raznovich (b. 1945), Jorge Goldenberg (b. 1941), and Mauricio Kartun (b. 1946) as well as Ricardo Monti (b. 1944).

During the 1970s it became clear that the theme of *El avión negro* was no longer far-fetched; Perón did, in fact, return to the country in 1973 for the last nine months of his life, until his death on July 1, 1974. At that time, power was placed in the hands of his wife, Isabel. From 1973 to 1976, when the country experienced a period of relative cultural freedom, there was nonetheless scant notable theatrical production. Among the few plays of note is Eduardo Pavlovsky's *El señor Galíndez*, a play dealing with torture in Argentina. The play was an eerie foreshadowing of the violence that would pervade the country under the pretext of nation building from 1976 to 1983 (Taylor 1997, 172).

On March 24, 1976, the government of Isabel Perón was overthrown, and the country once again returned to a dictatorship, one of the bloodiest of its history, the Process of National Reorganization, or *Proceso*, which lasted until 1983. In spite of the dictatorship, or possibly because of it, Argentine theater experienced a positive upswing in terms of creativity and quality. Although any direct references to the realities of the day were prohibited, playwrights were able to use metaphor to avoid censorship. They were forced to find codes that the public could understand but would pass unnoticed by the censors (never known for their mental prowess). There was, of necessity, much symbolism and use of elliptic language. Dramatists needed to be as creative as possible, and the results were excellent. Cossa, Gambarro, Gorostiza, Monti, Pavlovsky, Halac, Goldenberg, Bortnik, Mauricio, Raznovich, and Kartun all were able to present some of their greatest plays, which mixed realism and vanguardism and became uniquely Argentine. They were doing so in an increasingly chaotic situation in which uncertainty reigned and disappearances were a common occurrence.

Arguably one of the most important events in the history of Argentine theater began in 1981 with the Teatro Abierto, or Open Theater cycle. A group, organized by Osvaldo Dragún, wanted to present a response to the years of dictatorship. More than 300 theater practitioners joined forces, offering their work for free, in order to produce twenty-one brief plays, three per day, to an enthusiastic audience. The ramifications of the event cannot be underestimated. When one of the theaters in which the plays were going to be presented, el Teatro del Picadero, was destroyed by a fire set by those who felt threatened by the magnitude of the event, it only added to the cycle's popularity. Seventeen theaters immediately offered their own space for the plays that had been scheduled to be performed at the Picadero.

In 1982 the event was held again, but this time more than 300 aspiring dramatists entered a contest to determine which plays would be presented alongside the work of the well-known theater giants. After 1982 the Open Theater began to decline; the public was mobilized by the elections that would soon take place and by the disastrous attempt to regain the Falkland Islands. In 1983 the Open Theater had its final run, in which new plays by Kartun and Eduardo Rovner (1942) were staged, but in 1984 it was decided that the quality of work was not sufficient to warrant the cycle, and it was dissolved. Nonetheless, the Open Theater stands as a monument to the political strength of solidarity in the arts, and it left Argentina with an enriched national theater production.

Democracy returned to the country in December 1983 when Raúl Alfonsín assumed the presidency. Unfortunately, Argentina then lapsed into a period of economic decline that significantly impacted the theater. The economic situation and the return to uncensored television and movies contributed to a general lack of interest on the part of the Argentine public in the theater. In the wake of the new freedom of expression, the artistic community had lost its rallying point—the dictatorship. The motivation to write, the need to raise consciousness or connect in clever ways to the audience, was lost. Dramatists were left wondering what to write about now. Although inequities and social injustices still occurred, the playwrights did not seem to want to dwell on them. Eduardo Pavlovsky was possibly the dramatist best able to transmit the concerns of a postdictatorship Argentina—memory and forgetting, repression and freedom, and revenge and forgiveness. Gambaro, Cossa, Gorostiza, Kartun, Rovner, Dragún, and Monti were also able to write about the issues that concerned Argentine identity at that time.

The one thing that most Argentine playwrights had in common during the late 1980s was the rediscovery of the theater of Armando Discépolo and the *sainete* and the grotesque, the two genres he cultivated. There was in contemporary theater a vindication of so many of the elements that he used, such as the combinations of humor and cruelty and poetry. All of these components came to be used by authors in the 1980s.

In the 1990s, a new tendency emerged as a result of the increasingly dismal revelations concerning government corruption and the broken promises of elected officials. Language began to be seen as something that conveyed little meaning, and attention was now paid to image, sound, light, color, movement, and texture. Theater has been transformed into a multisensorial experience with elements of dance, rock music, circus performance, videos, popular folklore, and any other number of possible elements joined together. Numerous groups, such as la Organización negra, El Teatrito, and the now defunct Gambas al Ajillo, have presented these spectacles.

While these productions are generally categorized as the theater of youth culture or underground theater, their impact is being felt in the mainstream theater. An example of this would be the 1997 production, at the Centro Cultural San Martín, of Renata Schussheim and Oscar Araiz's *Boquitas pintadas* (Little painted mouths) by Manuel Puig. In the production, presented by the Contemporary Ballet of San Martín in 1997, a collage of elements was used, including modern dance, ballet, and a live radio show from the 1940s. One entire sequence of the show was seen as though one were watching a videotape rewinding, with all of the actors talking and moving in reverse. Another example of the influence of the youth culture would be the production of Diana Raznovich's *Máquinas divinas* (Divine machines) at the San Martín 1996 in which rock music and circus acrobatics take their place in the post-apocalyptic stage. Thus, it would seem, that Argentine theater, with its contemporary circuslike transformations and lively, eclectic spectacles, has in many ways returned to its own roots and come full circle.

REFERENCES

Arancibia, Juana A., and Zulema Mirkin, eds. *Teatro argentino durante el proceso (1976–1983)*. Buenos Aires: Editorial Vinciguerra, 1992.

Artaud, Antonin. *Theater and Its Double*. Trans. by Mary Caroline Richards. New York: Grove Press, 1958.

Azzi, María Susana. "The Golden Age and After: 1920s–1990s." In *Tango! The Dance, the Song, the Story*, edited by Simon Collier, Artemis Cooper, Susana Azzi, and Richard Martin, 114–60. London: Thames and Hudson, 1995.

Collier, Simon. "The Tango is Born: 1880s–1920s." In *Tango! The Dance, the Song, the Story*, edited by Simon Collier, Artemis Cooper, Susana Azzi, and Richard Martin, 18–64. London: Thames and Hudson, 1995.

Cooper, Artemis. "Tangomania in Europe and North America: 1913–1914." In *Tango! The Dance, the Song, the Story*, edited by Simon Collier, Artemis Cooper, Susana Azzi, and Richard Martin, 114–60. London: Thames and Hudson, 1995.

Evans, Judith. "The Sultry Tango." In *Insight Guides Argentina*. Ed. Deidre Ball. Singapore: APA Publications, 1988.

———. "Tango." In *Buenos Aires Insight Cityguides*, edited by Kathleen Wheaton, 147–50. Singapore: APA Publications, 1988.

Fernández, Gerardo. "Historias para ser contadas." In *Teatro argentino contemporáneo: Antología*. Coordinated by Gerardo Fernández, 13–63. Buenos Aires, Fondo de Cultura Económica, 1992.

Guy, Donna J. *Sex and Danger in Buenos Aires: Prostitution, Family and Nation*. Lincoln: University of Nebraska Press, 1991.

Pellarolo, Silvia. *Sainete criollo: democracia/representación. El caso de Nemesio Trejo*. Buenos Aires: Corregidor, 1997.

Pellettieri, Osvaldo. *Cien años de teatro argentino (1886–1990): Del Moreira a Teatro Abierto*. Buenos Aires: Galerna/IITCTL, 1990.

Perrottet, Anthony. "A Night at the Opera." In *Buenos Aires Insight Cityguides*, edited by Kathleen Wheaton, 124–26. Singapore: APA Publications, 1988.

Ross, Stanley R., and Thomas F. McGann, eds. *Buenos Aires: 400 Years*. Austin: University of Texas Press, 1982.

Taylor, Diana. *Disappearing Acts: Spectacles of Gender and Nationalism in Argentina's "Dirty War."* Durham, N.C.: Duke University Press, 1997.

Urquiza, Juan José de. *El Cervantes en la historia del teatro argentino*. Buenos Aires: Ediciones Culturales Argentinas, 1968.

8

Art (Painting, Sculpture, Photography)

ARGENTINA typically has been underrecognized for artistic achievement in spite of the fact that many Argentine plastic artists have earned international reputations for themselves. The contributions of Argentine artists to the larger body of Latin American art have been dwarfed by such giants as the Mexican muralists Diego Rivera, David Alfaro Siqueiros, and José Clemente Orozco; the pained artist cum pop icon Frida Kahlo from Mexico; the Colombian Fernando Botero; and others considered to be among the masters of Latin American art. Another factor that has contributed to the overshadowing of the visual arts in Argentina is the overwhelming dominance of literature on the cultural landscape. Notwithstanding this somewhat secondary status, the fine arts enjoy a solid infrastructure of first-rate museums and arts-oriented institutions.

In July 1895 President José Evaristo Uriburu signed a decree which put into motion the groundwork for the establishment of the Museo Nacional de Bellas Artes (National Museum of Fine Arts, or MNBA), which was inaugurated in December 1896. For more than 100 years the MNBA has housed the works of the country's finest artists, and it frequently hosts traveling exhibitions from foreign countries.

Argentina has a history of sustaining a large community of world-class artists, which continues today. The development and evolution of the plastic arts in Argentina have been closely linked to the same movements that influenced literature. In fact, most of the major artistic movements and groups were initiated and motivated by a broad range of artists. The two major artistic movements of the twentieth century were the Florida group, principally an aesthetic movement made up of upper-class elite, and the Boedo group, the socially committed bohemian school of the working class. Both groups included writers and plastic artists of every type. Corresponding to the Florida and Boedo groups were two other organizations with very similar perspectives. The Amigos del Arte (Friends of Art), established in 1924, was backed by government funding. It served as an artistic forum for the Buenos Aires elite, a place to go when one wanted to see and be seen. Those who were privileged enough to attend functions sponsored by the Amigos del Arte would find themselves mentioned in the society pages of *La Nación*, the conservative newspaper of the oligarchy. The organization showed art films, held chamber music concerts, and regularly featured art exhibitions; it also brought in famous intellectuals from Europe and the Americas to lecture. The more avant-garde group Signo, founded in 1933, was a neutral home to a diverse gathering of high-profile writers, artists, and musicians, including Jorge Luis Borges, Norah Lange, Raúl González Tuñón, Oliverio Girondo, Xul Solar, Antonio Berni, Juan Carlos Paz, José María Castro, and Luis Gianneo.

The next most significant boom of artistic activity and innovation did not come until after the fall of Perón in 1955. In 1958 the Instituto Di Tella was established by two brothers, Torcuato and Guido Di Tella. Their father, who had earned a fortune as an industrialist, was a generous philanthropist and patron of the arts. The institute housed three main branches dedicated to the promotion of fine arts, theater, and music. The Instituto Di Tella was located at the center of virtually all aspects of the arts in the 1960s. It recruited the top people as administrators and aggressively promoted national and international art and artists. In spite of the huge successes and the advancements made by the Di Tella, by 1967 and 1968 the resurgence of political and economic upheaval was taking its toll. By 1970 the foundation that supported the Instituto Di Tella was embroiled in internal disputes, and, bankrupt, it was forced to end all operations. One year prior to the closing of the Di Tella, however, Jorge Glusberg founded the Centro de Arte y Comunicaciones (Center for Art and Communications, or CAYC). The CAYC picked up where the Di Tella had left off and became the major artistic institution from 1970 to 1975. It promoted the fusion of the arts with technology and science. One of the most important artists to come out of the CAYC was Luis Benedit (b. 1937).

While Argentina is home to many artists who have been at the forefront of the successive movements and development of the plastic arts, several stand out for their significant contributions and the roles they have played in shaping the artistic heritage of the country.

PAINTING

Florencio Molina Campos

The art of Florencio Molina Campos (1891–1959) has made a lasting impression in Argentina and abroad. His popular charicaturesque drawings of rural life and gauchos are readily identifiable, and they have earned him a reputation as one of Argentina's foremost artists. As a boy, Molina Campos spent many of his vacations on his father's ranch, Los Angeles, in El Tuyú and also at La Matilde, the ranch his family leased in the province of Entre Ríos. Here, the young artist began to sketch the rural people and places that later would constitute his life's work. Molina Campos worked at a number of odd jobs—including employment with the Post Office and the Sociedad Rural—and he led a rather unsettled life before he established a niche for himself as a full-time professional artist. His first break came in 1926 when a selection of his works was exhibited at the Sociedad Rural's annual fair and livestock show in Buenos Aires. The exhibition coincided with the publication of Ricardo Güiraldes's *Don Segundo Sombra* that same year. President Marcelo T. de Alvear visited the show and was so struck by Molina Campos's works that he purchased two for himself. The artist gained almost instant notoriety, and the remainder of his paintings quickly sold. The same year he was offered a position by the Colegio Nacional Nicolás Avellaneda to teach art.

With subsequent exhibitions at the Feria Rural and elsewhere, Molina Campos's fame and status as a artist flourished. Nevertheless, it was his contract with the Fábrica Argentina de Alpargatas (Argentine Alpargatas [traditional footwear] Factory), which hired him to illustrate the company's calendar, that placed his work into the homes of countless Argentines of all social classes and made him the most widely recognized artist in the country. His Alpargatas paintings are his most famous. The calendar ran from 1931 to 1936, with a second series between 1940 and 1945. Each month's painting was accompanied by a brief narrative description of the scene, carefully written to mimic rural speech patterns. His drawings also appeared in the popular magazine *Caras y caretas* in Argentina, as well as in *Fortune, Esquire, Time, Life, Saturday Evening Post*, and *National Geographic* in the United States. In 1942 the Kraft publishing house in Buenos Aires published a now famous and hard to obtain edition of the satirical gauchesque poem *Fausto* (1866)—written by Estanislao del Campo (1834–1880)—with illustrations by Molina Campos.

Molina Campos lived in the United States for several years after receiving a grant to study animation. He lived in the Los Angeles area where he worked for Walt Disney as a consultant and planned an animated film based on his drawings. He became disillusioned by what he felt was Disney's denigration of the gaucho image and left. However, his works were exhibited in numerous galleries such as the San Francisco Museum of Art, the Laguna Beach Art Gallery, the University of California at Los Angeles, Pomona College, and Claremont College. He also illustrated calendars, of farm machinery, for a Minnesota manufacturer (Minneapolis Moline) from 1944 to 1958. These calendars, like those he had done in Argentina, became famous throughout the country. Richard Nixon, who had met the artist in Buenos Aires in 1958, owned several Molina Campos paintings. In 1959 the Tinker Foundation, which was established in Texas, sponsored a large exhibition of his works. Molina Campos died on November 16 of that same year. The Molina Campos Foundation was inaugurated in 1969 in Argentina, and in 1979 his second wife, María Elvira Ponce Aguirre de Molina, founded a museum dedicated to her late husband in the provincial town of Moreno.

It can be said that Molina Campos achieved in painting what such authors as José Hernández (1834–1886), Benito Lynch (1880–1951), and Ricardo Güiraldes (1886–1927) accomplished in literature: the transformation of the figure of the rogue gaucho into a positive national symbol and a hallmark of Argentine identity. This image of the gaucho is at the very core of Argentine national character. Certainly, Molina Campos was not the first artist to depict the rugged Argentine plainsmen, but his work was uniquely original in its execution. His caricatures of gauchos and country folk, as well as their animals and environment, elicit humor in the observer; however, upon closer inspection, his paintings reveal the artist's attention to detail and his great admiration for his subjects. The paintings depict a positive, lovable image of the gaucho as honorable, courageous, resolute, and perhaps above all hardworking, in much the same vein as Hernández's character Martín Fierro and Güiraldes's Don Segundo Sombra.

While Molina Campos's vision of the gaucho is not that of the nineteenth-century roaming outlaw, neither is it one that errs on the side of exaggerating the heroic, even Homeric, feats of the gaucho, which, for example, is so passionately argued for in Leopoldo Lugones's (1874–1938) *El payador* (1916). Rather, the artist sought to paint an accurate and simultaneously whimsical representation of the quotidian world of the country people who inhabited the marginal rural outreaches of Argentine society, so often overshadowed by the urban culture of metropolitan Buenos Aires. The result is a graphic record of extraordinary breadth which not only provides a visual sociological commentary, but also yields a sort of anthropological registry of traditional country customs, dress, conduct, and artifacts.

He dressed his subjects in every type of traditional clothing, from military uniforms to carnival costumes. Most impressive, however, are his visual renderings of traditional gaucho attire which he laboriously recreated down to the smallest detail and in surprising variety; no two of his gauchos are dressed alike. Although most of his figures are men, he also painted many women, including the typical *china* (country woman), schoolteachers, and brides, children, Italian organ grinders, and a good number of Afro-Argentines, who by and large had been erased from other registers of Argentine cultural identity.

Even though his style of painting can be described as caricature for the way in which physical traits, particularly facial features, are exaggerated, or magnified as if one were viewing them through a thick glass, the paintings do not reflect the mockery often associated with caricature. The embellished features underscore the emotional expression of the figures rather than distort them into ridiculous lampoons. Moreover, Molina Campos achieved an almost photographic realism in the way he positioned his figures, in their gestures, stance, and attitude. In several of his paintings, in fact, the people are posed as if for a photograph, staring out uncomfortably at the observer. The artist's use of light and shadow also provides in many of the paintings a remarkable sense of depth and proportion. Molina Campos is best described as a *costumbrista* artist for the manner in which he detailed scenes of local flavor and color. In this way, his art visually resembles the *costumbrista* writing of many nineteenth-century authors who "painted" the minutiae of everyday life with words. In the manner of literature, Molina Campos featured a recurring protagonist, by the name of Tiléforo Areco, whose life is chronicled by scenes of his engagement, wedding, and the birth of his first child.

Second only to the humans who populate his paintings is the assortment of animals he drew: horses, cattle, sheep, dogs, cats, all manner of farm fowl, even rats, parrots, and monkeys. Most notable among his animal creations are the horses, the ever-faithful and always present companions of gaucho and farmhand. Molina Campos created a diverse gallery of the native horse of the Pampas; with every possible color and coat pattern, each and every horse is unique. What they all have in common is their bulging eyes which give them an attentive, almost frenzied appearance. The horses often reflect in their own expression that of their rider or driver, whether it be determination, courage, weariness, or wonder.

Molina Campos also paid great attention to his representation of the natural world and man's place in it. His landscapes depict virtually every physical aspect of the Pampas from wetlands to the vast expanses of prairie—the blazing sun, a starry night, or a driving storm—from cattails to the huge *ombú* (gigantic bush). Likewise, he painted a compendium of rural architecture including the rustic dwellings of the country folk, ranch buildings, train stations, *pulperías* (general stores), and schoolhouses.

It is worth noting that, although Molina Campos dedicated the focus of his work to the most humble sector of Argentine society, he was rather unidimensional in his portrayal of the people who inhabited his paintings. He seems to have chosen to paint what could be perceived as the benefits and virtues of the country lifestyle. He created a kind of pictorial celebration of the simple way of life extolled in depictions of people sharing *mate* around a fire, gauchos engaged in typical demonstrations of skill such as the game of *pato*, groups of people celebrating a holiday or simply gathered at the local *pulpería*. Even his paintings of people hard at work or of weathered gauchos enduring a storm speak to the virtues of honest labor and long-suffering. What is conspicuously absent from the paintings is any vision of suffering or true poverty. His figures are humble and poor, but they seem content with their lot in life and manifest no obvious complaints regarding their social status nor their bleak existence on the fringes of mainstream society.

Molina Campos's paintings are enhanced by the use of delicate humor which conjures up a feeling of nostalgia in the observer for a bygone era. His works preserve the rural soul of the country, whether real or imagined, and communicate the foibles of human nature. They are unique in that they adhere to no particular school of painting nor do they pretend to espouse any particular political agenda. His work is oddly positioned somewhere between graphic humor and high art, and as such it has become somewhat of a pop icon. It has become fashionable in the last several years to own a Molina Campos. Prints and reproductions can be purchased in high-priced galleries and in used-book stores. Perhaps for this reason the work of no other Argentine artist before or since has achieved such a central position in and made such a lasting impression on the national cultural consciousness.

Xul Solar

Oscar Alejandro Agustín Schulz Solari (1887–1963), better known by the name he used to sign his works, Xul Solar, was the most prominent Argentine artist during the first half of the twentieth century. He began his career by studying art in Europe between 1912 and 1924. When he returned to Buenos Aires, he became involved with the *martínfierrista* group of intellectuals. It was during this time that he met Jorge Luis Borges, who would become one of his closest friends throughout his life. Solar's work represents the fast-paced urban culture of Buenos Aires, a cosmopolitan city caught up in the process of rapid modernization. The artist himself is the product of the new Argentina, shaped largely by foreign influence and massive immigration; his father emigrated from Germany and his mother from Italy. Solar's art mirrored the changing cultural landscape of Argentina.

Xul Solar was an avid student of world religions, philosophy, astrology, and the occult. He spent his life in the pursuit of knowledge and a universal religious principle. This hunger to uncover meaning in human existence and the relationship of man to the vastness of the universe completely occupied his life, and it is consequently reflected in his extraordinary artwork. He was renowned among his peers because he refused to accept the tangible and visible in life as the limits of reality, but he was most cherished as a person of exceeding generosity and kindness. Aside from his painting and studies, he considered himself to be a creator of sorts. He developed a game known as *panajedrez* (panchess) and a universal language based on numerology and astrology, *panlengua* (panlanguage). Similarly, he claimed to have created a new language for Latin America called *neocriollo* (neocreole) based on the commonalities between Spanish and Portuguese. He even published some of his writing in *neocriollo*. In addition, Xul Solar took up architecture and sketched several fanciful projects which he placed in Tigre, a development on the Paraná River outside of Buenos Aires where traditionally the wealthy retreat. His architectural designs were created based on his conception of the Kabbalah. All of his activities and interests, however, revolve around astrology, the lens through which he viewed the relationship among all things.

Solar's presence in the artistic milieu of Buenos Aires was so prominent that his life literally became the stuff of fiction. Roberto Arlt (1900–1942) shared the same immigrant origins as Solar, and in many ways the two men were similar, primarily in their shared affinity for astrology, mysticism, and alchemy. It is not difficult to make a comparison between Arlt's famous character, el Astrólogo (in his novel *Los siete locos* [1929]) and the astrologer Solar. Likewise, in his famous literary recreation of Buenos Aires, *Adán Buenosayres* (1948), Leopoldo Marechal (1900–1979) included Solar as the thinly disguised astrologer Schultze, one of the main protagonists.

Solar's painting, like Arlt's and Marechal's fiction, depicts the chaos resulting from the struggle going on between the traditional and the avantgarde in Argentina. The almost violent thrust of modernity comes through in his work in the form of geometrical shapes, fantastic beings, scientific and religious symbology, and imaginary and unforeseen spaces. His paintings do not tell stories; they are constructed as equations of semiotic markers that produce a visual allegory for interpreting the changing social face of Argentina and its citizens. A recurring theme in many of his paintings is that of the voyage or quest, represented by roads, walkways, and ladders leading up mountain sides, to shrines, or at times into nothingness, an abyss or a void. His work, which spans some forty-five years, can be divided into three periods.

His early period began with his experience in Europe and the formation of his identity as an artist. The paintings from this period are characterized by the use of sharply defined geometric shapes, bright colors, and what one might call fantasies or dreamscapes. While he was in Europe he created his first architectural designs as expressionistic utopias. Toward the end of the first period, Solar began to incorporate letters, religious symbols, more political symbols, such as flags, and mythical creatures.

The second period began approximately in 1930 and lasted until 1960. During this time, there was an increased focus on the esoteric, and his paintings took on a decidedly more spiritual character. In the early 1940s, he began a period of painting in black and white. Likewise, it was during this period that architecture became central to his work. His paintings are mainly of buildings, imaginary cities, futuristic scenes, and even extraplanetary spaces.

The third and final period, which began around 1960, is marked by a return to vivid colors as well as the incorporation of a new set of symbols and calligraphy. Many of these paintings present clearly organized sets of symbols, similar to Egyptian hieroglyphics, that beckon the observer to interpret the hidden meaning concealed in their arrangement. An identifiable alphabet of symbols is recognizable throughout. Also famous from this period are his portraits of Jesus Christ and Moses, among other, more secular figures.

Xul Solar remains best remembered and admired for the paintings he completed during the 1920s and 1930s, a time of social change and upheaval in Argentina. His works stands as an artistic response to the debate over the nature of culture and the question of nationality during this pivotal time in the country's history.

Raquel Forner

Raquel Forner (1902–1988) began her career as an artist with studies at the Academia Nacional de Bellas Artes (National Academy of Fine Arts) in Buenos Aires, where she earned a degree as an art professor. Like so many others of her generation, she traveled to Europe to expand her artistic vision. From 1929 to 1931 she studied in Paris with Émile Othon Friesz. She is most known for her dramatic paintings that depict the atrocities and consequences of the Spanish Civil War and later World War II. As the daughter of Spanish immigrants to Argentina, she maintained an intimate connection with her Iberian heritage. She is considered to be the first practitioner of expressionism in Argentina with her clearly existential perspective and her characteristically phantasmagoric figures. In her art one can perceive the influence of a wide range of other artists and styles, from El Greco to Pablo Picasso.

Forner worked in a very concentrated manner, creating whole series of paintings that revolved around a given theme. Among her best-known earlier works are those of the *Serie de el drama* (Drama series). They are dark, somber portrayals of a world torn asunder by violence and rage. Representative of the series are *Amanecer* (Dawn, 1944) and *El juicio* (The judgement, 1946) in which the central figures are women all with the same pained expression in their hollow eyes. The paintings are like great epic tales with smaller scenes surrounding the focal point of the painting. These secondary representations depict both despair and hope. Torn bodies simultaneously return to and spring from the earth as symbolic images which seem to speak of the cycle of human existence in a chaotic world.

In the 1960s and 1970s Forner's work was dominated by her fascination with space travel, particularly as a manifestation of mankind's eternal voyage. Her interest in space exploration was not merely figurative. She took a great interest in what it meant for humanity to break free of earthly confinement. In 1974 she visited NASA in Houston. During this time, she painted her Space series, which included *Serie de los astronautas* (Astronaut series) and *Serie de las mutaciones espaciales* (Space mutant series). In these abstract visions of man's adventure in space astronauts come into, sometimes perilous, contact with a variety of space beings and space fauna and mutants. In addition to contact with extraterrestrial beings, Forner painted visions of what future earth dwellers—hybrid creatures—might look like. Some of her paintings belong to the collection of the National Air and Space Museum in Washington D.C.

Antonio Berni

Those artists who belonged to the Boedo group, like their counterpart writers, were clearly politically and socially motivated. They sought to portray the downtrodden sectors of society realistically and reveal the mechanisms of oppression that marginalized them. Painters in this group included José Arato (1893–1939) and Adolfo Bellocq (1899–1972). However, perhaps the most famous Argentine painter whose art is associated with issues of social justice is Antonio Berni (1905–1981). Berni was not a member of the Boedo group, but he was undoubtedly influenced by their work and their social commitment. He picked up where the Boedo artists left off and pioneered what is known as *nuevo realismo* or *neorrealismo* (new realism), which had an obviously impressionistic quality to it.

Berni aligned himself politically and ideologically with communism, particularly with the plight of the common laborer. His paintings demonstrate his commitment to social change and to his clear vision of the artist as an agent for such change, much like the great Mexican muralists. Indeed, Berni met David Alfaro Siquieros on the latter's visit to Buenos Aires in 1933 and worked with him rather closely. During this time Berni had the opportunity to discuss with Siqueiros his vision of the function of art and its role in social revolution. Berni's murals can be seen in the Teatro del Pueblo, the Galerías Pacífico (recently converted into an upscale shopping center on Florida Avenue), and the Sociedad Hebraica Argentina.

As an artist of the people, Berni attempted to portray a wide range of the working class from all regions of Argentina. His paintings have as subjects neighborhood soccer matches, typical tango orchestras, and scenes of country life and the existence of those who inhabit the *villas miserias* (slums). He painted the urban, largely immigrant population of Buenos Aires as well as the marginalized mainly indigenous people of such provinces as Jujuy in the far north. A great number of his paintings, however, depict unemployment, strikes, and the exploitation of laborers, from miners and factory workers to the *golondrinas*, or migrant farmworkers (the name literally means "swallows"), most of whom were Italians who came to Argentina during harvest season and then returned to Italy when the work was over.

Around 1960 Berni began to exhibit a change in his style of artistic expression, but his commitment to social justice seemed stronger than ever. The artist moved away from the neorealist style of painting and began to experiment with collage. He collected objects and debris from the *villas miserias* and used them to recreate scenes from the same slums, thus literally uniting his subject with his art. Berni's collages constituted strong social statements about the social predicament of Argentina's lumpen class. The innovative medium of his work, together with the social aspect, made the collages extremely popular.

Another factor that contributed to the popularity of the collages was Berni's creation of two protagonists who frequently appeared in the paintings: Juanito Laguna and Ramona Montiel. Viewed collectively, the collages of these characters can be read as narratives of their lives and, of course, on a grander scale of Argentina itself. One can see Juanito engaged in a variety of activities including flying his kite, sitting by the pond, or just watching television. One of the more arresting paintings in the Juanito series is that of the boy standing in the middle of the slum and looking upward at an astronaut in a space capsule passing overhead. The painting is a clever juxtaposition of the First and Third World, and it points rather eloquently to the huge gap separating the two. Likewise, one can follow the path of Ramona's life as an innocent and poverty-stricken girl, working at odd jobs from seamstress to prostitute. Ramona is most often seen surrounded by male authority figures who exploit her. The Juanito and Ramona series made such an impact on the collective Argentine consciousness that they gave rise to a whole series of secondary artistic expressions. This was particularly the case with the figure of Juanito Laguna, about whom a number of popular songs and tangos were written (Troche and Gassiot-Talabot 1971, 62). During the 1970s, most specifically during the military dictatorship, Berni used collage to create a number of horrific works in which he depicted scenes of torture and abuse being carried out by the military government.

Berni is by any standard one of Argentina's most memorable artists, and his works have not only become part of the national cultural heritage, they are among the most valuable. In fact, in November 1997, Berni's painting *La gallina ciega* (The blind hen, 1972), depicting a group of children playing the game for which it is titled, was sold at auction by Christie's in New York City for more than $600,000, making it the highest priced work in the history of Argentine art.

The Silhouettes

There does not exist in Argentina a popular form of art associated with the years of military repression such as the *arpilleras* (works made of burlap with stitched figures) in Chile. However, in the early 1980s, there did surface in Argentina a clandestine yet extremely public form of artistic expression in response to the years of terrorism waged by the military against the citizenry and the consequent "disappearance" of thousands of individuals. In Buenos Aires, as well as in other major cities of the interior, there began to appear in ever-increasing numbers the outlines of human bodies, silhouettes of those who had been disappeared. They were painted on walls and streets, in plazas, and other public spaces. Sometimes they were accompanied by the name of a person and the date of his or her disappearance. The visual impact of these haunting images, like ghosts wandering among the living in the public domain, was tremendous. The political message was an overt defiance of the military's waning authority. The anonymous artists successfully turned the most public spaces into exhibitions that could not go unnoticed. This manifestation of communal conceptual art gave form to the unseen and a voice to the unspoken. A discussion of the silhouettes as art and a classification of the variations have been undertaken by R. A. Cerisola. The silhouettes have become a permanent part of the Plaza de Mayo where the Mothers of the Plaza de Mayo continue to march each Thursday.

MIXED MEDIA

Luis Benedit

Luis Benedit (1937) is perhaps one of the most eclectic contemporary Argentine artists. He was educated as an architect, a profession he continues to exercise, but never underwent any formal training as an artist. In addition to his painting, Benedit is famous for his habitats, installations, and sculptures.

Benedit's first works relied heavily upon their relationship to scientific experimentation and an analysis of animal behavior. In 1968 he exhibited his complex installation known as the *Microzoo* in one of the most sophisticated artistic spaces of the period, the Galería Rubbers. *Microzoo* comprised a series of minihabitats in which a wide variety of animals and plants were placed on show for observation by the public. The habitats housed cats, birds, ants, fish, turtles, bees, and a number of other creatures as well as plants in various stages of germination and growth. The installation had a clearly ecological purpose to acquaint the public with the multiple microcosms of the animal and plant kingdoms.

In 1970 Benedit was selected to represent Argentina at the Venice Biennale where he exhibited, to critical acclaim, his installation *Biotrón*, a massive acrylic enclosure containing 4,000 live bees that had the choice of feeding on artificial flowers that produced "nectar" or on the live flowers in the gardens to which they were connected. In 1972 his *Fitotrón* ("Phytotron"), a complex hydroponic installation with an accompanying labyrinth for rats, was displayed at the Museum of Modern Art in New York City. These exhibitions were followed by a number of "projects" dealing with animals. One of the most famous of these was his *Proyecto huevos* (Eggs project, 1976), in which a chicken was presented as having been transformed by man from its natural state into a mere egg-producing mechanism.

His work during the late 1970s and early 1980s is predominated by a series known as *Los dibujos de Tomás* (Thomas's drawings). Benedit utilized his son's drawings as the basis for recreating a child's vision of art by both repainting Tomas's original and sculpting a three-dimensional version of it. Typical of this period are numerous representations of King Kong.

By the 1980s Benedit had established a reputation for himself as one of the most innovative artists working in Argentina. During this time he created a number of paintings and sculptures which have since become, to some extent, the hallmark of his work. They constitute an anthology dedicated to the art of the knife duel, a longtime symbol of Creole tradition and the gaucho heritage, reworked into abstract modern representations. There is also an intersection of his work with literature on this theme; the primary example is his 1991 sculpture of a large knife pierced by two smaller ones, which is mounted on a wooden box. The work is titled *El encuentro (Del informe de Brodie)* (The encounter from Brodie's Report). A drawer in the box contains another knife along with shredded pieces of the book *El informe de Brodie* (Brodie's report, 1970) by Jorge Luis Borges. Some of Benedit's other works pay homage to the literary characters Martín Fierro and his companion Cruz.

Benedit's works on dueling are part of even a larger project which has been the artist's focus since the 1980s when he began to incorporate images of Argentina's past into his works as a way of interpreting the present. He has accomplished this by pursuing two main avenues of historico-cultural restoration.

One of these is his collection of mixed-media works titled *Del viaje del Beagle*, based on naturalist Charles Darwin's voyage to the southern extensions of Argentina in the nineteenth century in the H.M.S. *Beagle* to catalogue and study the local flora and fauna. Benedit's works in this category include paintings and sketches of regional wildlife as well as indigenous human inhabitants. He also produced a number of sculptures and even furniture pieces inspired by Darwin's trip.

Benedit's most impressive work, however, is inspired by the rural past of Argentina with particular emphasis on the culture of the cattle industry. In 1989 Benedit helped organize a major exhibition of the works of Molina Campos for the Museum of Fine Arts in Buenos Aires. From this experience came a series of paintings inspired by the great *costumbrista* (artist). The paintings are recognizable abstract reformulations of Molina Campos's originals; many of them bear the same title, such as *Igualito a su tata* (Just like his dad, 1989). Other works that invoke Argentina's rural roots include his paintings of farm animals, his recreations of typical rural dwellings such as a farmhouse made out of sugar cubes, his sculptures of gauchos roping and branding cattle, the ranch implements used for tasks like dehorning and castrating displayed in decorative hand-crafted wooden cases, the spacious

installation titled *Marcas* (Brands, 1991) which showcases a number of famous cattle brands, and sculptures of gaucho attire (*Alpargata* [Boot] 1990)
and weapons (*Boleadoras*, 1990). Benedit's modernized reconceptualization
of these cultural artifacts updates them and reintroduces the past into the
cultural consciousness in a new light. The ingenuity of Benedit lies in his
always innovative ability to use common objects and lore as forums for interpretations of identity.

Since the return to democracy in 1983, Argentina has enjoyed a steady
increase in artistic activity made possible by the return of cultural freedom
and an improved economy. The opening of new galleries, together with the
creation of new foundations and prizes, has opened new venues for promising
young artists. One of the best indexes of the new generation of artists in
Argentina is to be found in the publication of the Museo Nacional de Bellas
Artes's *Premios Colección Costantini*, which showcases sixty-eight award-
winning artists and their works.

Mirta Kupferminc

Mirta Kupferminc (b. 1955) belongs to the generation of artists who began
gaining national attention and earning prestigious national and international
awards in the 1980s. She has continued to make a name for herself throughout the current decade with exhibitions of her works in the United States,
Europe, Asia, and Israel. Her works reflect the difficult and often violent
recent history of the country. Some of her most outstanding works are inspired by Jewish themes. She was commissioned to design a monument to
the memory of the victims of the 1994 bombing of the building of the
Asociación Mutual Israelita Argentina (Jewish Mutual Aid Society). The
monument, finished in 1996, can be found in the Plaza Lavalle in downtown
Buenos Aires.

PHOTOGRAPHY

Photography has been an important artistic and documentary medium in
Argentina since the mid-nineteenth century. The daguerreotype, predecessor
of the modern photograph, became extremely popular almost immediately
following its introduction into Argentina, which came by way of Uruguay.
Word of the amazing technique spread rapidly and everyone was eager to
have their picture made. Likewise, journalists discovered an incredible visual
way to document their stories. In spite of the daguerreotype's popularity, its
usefulness was short lived and it was soon replaced by the advanced tech-

nology of the photograph. During the 1860s Buenos Aires was literally teeming with photographers, most of whom were French, who were known as *fotógrafos pintores* (photographer painters) and specialized in portraiture. Their name came from the fact that their specialty was to create beautiful pictures of people by using such techniques as retouching, shadowing, or manipulating the lens and focus to detract from the less appealing features of the person being photographed.

Benito Panunzi

Buenos Aires had reached such a point of saturation of photographic artists that many began to venture into the nearby provinces and even farther in search of new opportunities. One of the most famous of these adventurers was Benito Panunzi (1819?–1887?). He was an experienced Italian photographer who, before arriving in Argentina in 1862, had traveled to India and China taking photographs. In Argentina, Panunzi set out to document the lives of the rapidly disappearing indigenous populations and the few authentic gauchos who yet remained. He also took photographs of Buenos Aires, which today are important records for documenting the original layout of the city. He established a photography business in Buenos Aires but abandoned the city in 1868. Panunzi's most famous photographs are stored at the Biblioteca Municipal Manuel Gálvez (Facio 1995, 12–13).

Alejandro S. Whitcomb

The most famous Argentine-born photographer of the nineteenth century was Alejandro S. Whitcomb (1835–1905). Whitcomb is responsible for documenting many different aspects of nineteenth-century life in Argentina, from the city to the farthest reaches of the outback and from the elite to the very poorest. In Buenos Aires he was the chosen photographer among society's well-to-do, and he photographed several of the nation's presidents and their families. In stark contrast are his portraits of half-dressed indigenous families taken on his trips to the interior of the country. He is also famous for his landscape photography and documentation of local customs and traditions.

Francisco Ayerza

Photography became so popular around the turn of the century that different organizations, clubs, and societies began to form. One of the earliest and most important of them was La Sociedad Fotográfica Argentina de Aficionados (Argentine Society of Amateur Photographers), which was established in 1889 by Francisco Ayerza (1860–1901) and directed by Leonardo Pereira. Their goal was to record and preserve through photography the daily life of both the city and the rural areas. Ayerza took a particular interest in documenting the traditional life of the gaucho and of country folk in general. His pictures are valuable resources today for observing conventional dress and manners. Among the most famous of Ayerza's photos is the series taken to illustrate an edition of José Hernández's epic gauchesque poem *Martín Fierro* (Facio 1995, 34).

Photography as an Artistic Medium

By the 1920s, photography had become a booming industry and had begun to develop into an artistic medium, moving away from the merely functional or documentary. In 1921 *Correo fotográfico sudamericano* (South American Photography Post), a periodical dedicated solely to the art of photography, was launched. It ran advertisements and published the artistic work of different photographers. The newspapers *La Prensa* (The press) and *La Nación* (The nation) also began to print photographic art in their Sunday supplements. Other photography publications began to surface in the 1930s.

Photographic Journalism

During the first three decades of the twentieth century, photographic journalism matured due in large part to the remarkably popular journal *Caras y caretas*, which was published from 1898 to 1939. *Caras y caretas* featured photojournalism sections with photographs documenting an event with captions of text next to them. The visual record of stories that ranged from war to natural disasters to society events took precedence over the written word.

By the 1960s photography had developed into a sophisticated art form as well as an invaluable component of journalism. In the journalist's hands, the camera had become a weapon against corruption and injustice; consequently, it increased the danger of the job. In Argentina, as elsewhere in Latin America, journalism can be a risky profession with the very real threat of losing one's life. During the turbulent years from 1966 to 1983, with subsequent military takeovers and political and economic upheaval in general, photography suffered some of its darkest years. During the *Proceso de Reorganización Nacional* (1976–1983), photography literally became an underground activity because photographers had to contend with censorship, lack of journalistic freedom, and threats from the military. Virtually every photographer was subject to suspicion by the military government, even those who were allowed to work for the approved newspapers and cover official events. The very act of carrying a camera in public could be considered a subversive and criminal act (Facio 1993, 270). In spite of the imminent danger, many photographers continued to document the atrocities as well as the arrogance of the military government. These photographs, however, did not begin to surface until around 1981 when the demise of the dictatorship began to be perceived by the public and censorship was not as strictly enforced. It was during this time that some of the first pictures of the Mothers of the Plaza de Mayo appeared. The return to democracy in 1983 made possible many different photographic exhibitions in which the whole truth of the dictatorship began to be revealed with documentary clarity.

One of the most moving photo essays on the topic of the dictatorship is the widely distributed *Democracia vigilada: fotógrafos argentinos* (Eye on democracy: Argentine photographers, 1988), edited by Pablo Ortiz Monasterio. The photographs cover the eleven years from 1975 to 1986. The photographers include Eduardo Longoni, one of the most famous chroniclers of the *Proceso* known especially for his photographs of military officials, Jorge Aguirre, Silvio Zuccheri, Rafael Wollman, and Marcelo Ranea. Wollman is known for his photographs of the Malvinas or Falkland Islands War. He did not go to the Malvinas to cover the war; he was already there taking shots of the local flora and fauna. Since journalists and photographers were immediately prohibited from traveling to the islands to document to war, Wollman's photos are some of the very few taken by an Argentine photographer (Facio 1993, 276). The images that make up the photographic essay are compelling for the way in which they chronicle the period and capture a wide gamut of events and emotions. One of the most fascinating aspects of the volume is how it presents the relationship between the military and the Catholic Church. The first photograph is one of General Videla kneeling in prayer while the priest serves communion to a young boy. Others show priests, nuns, and even Monseñor Casaroli, often with military officials within arms' reach. Another group of photos shows soldiers and policemen engaged in crowd control and even beating or dragging away protestors. One of the most poignant images, however, is that of a policeman and one of the Mothers of the Plaza de Mayo in a mutual embrace. The most disturbing photographs show the forensic evidence used in the trials against the generals: piles of exhumed bones or the image of a skull projected onto a courtroom screen. In sum, *Democracia vigilada* stands as an effective testimony to the power of photography as a form of communication.

In the years following the return to democracy, photography in Argentina has blossomed to meet its full artistic potential. One of the premier permanent galleries in Buenos Aires is the Fotogalería of the Centro Cultural General San Martín, which opened in 1985. Since its inauguration, the Fotogalería has sponsored well over 100 photography exhibitions from around the world and Argentina. The gallery organizes historic exhibitions of Argentine photography and showcases new talent.

Sara Facio and Alicia D'Amico

For more than thirty years, Sara Facio (b. 1932) and her former collaborator Alicia D'Amico (b. 1933) were a permanent fixture of photography in Argentina. Their work has been fundamental to the advancement of the art and the social function of photography. Facio and D'Amico opened a studio together in 1960 and worked arduously as professional photographers, sponsors of specialized organizations, journalists, historians, and book editors. They organized countless exhibitions. In sum, together, and now separately, they have contributed to virtually every facet of the photography industry in Argentina, and they have made a lasting impact as leaders, promoters, and artists.

Facio and D'Amico were particularly interested in creating photography collections in book form. They are famous for their photo essays of the late 1960s and 1970s, such as *Buenos Aires Buenos Aires* (1968), which portrays every aspect of the city with intensity and honesty; it also contains texts written by Julio Cortázar. Later similar collections include *Retratos y autorretratos* (Portraits and self-portraits, 1973), with photos of over twenty Latin American writers with accompanying text, and *Humanario* (Humanary, 1976), an exploration of the world of the mentally insane with commentary by Cortázar. The photographs from *Humanario* were exhibited in Houston, Texas, in 1992.

Facio and D'Amico have not worked collaboratively since 1985, but both have continued zealously with individual projects. Facio currently is the director of the Fotogalería of the Teatro Municipal General San Martín and she heads La Azotea, a publishing house dedicated to photography.

Eduardo Gil

The photography of Eduardo Gil (b. 1948) is especially representative of work done since the return to constitutional democracy in 1983. Gil, a professional photographer, is most known for the superb work he has done for travel guides, including the Latin American volumes in the *Insight* series. He is also an art photographer, and most of his black-and-white works are the antithesis of his tourist images. The black-and-white works focus overtly on a gritty texture of urban realism that belies tourist images of Argentina, especially those that echo propositions about Buenos Aires as the Paris of the Southern Hemisphere, the sophistication in dress and social custom, and the much touted prosperity to be witnessed in the streets of Buenos Aires.

With his studio located in one of the city's old and rundown fringe districts, only a few blocks from the main government plaza, Gil has specialized in what one might call a studied intrusive lens into daily life. This is particularly evident in his series on institutionalized mental patients, which raises interesting ethical questions about the invasion of privacy and nonconsenting dispositions of human bodies. However, institutionalized individuals are at the disposal of the state, and it is this disposibility that Gil is interested in examining.

Street scenes are another of Gil's preferred topics. He emphasizes the dirty realism of daily life, which has been a recurring theme in other forms of cultural production in Argentina such as the novel, the theater, and film. The harsh angles and stares of his subjects tend to belie the urbaneness that is a recurring motif of the myth of *Porteño* sophistication.

REFERENCES

Campo, Estanislao del. *Fausto*. Con ilustraciones del costumbrista Florencio Molina Campos. Buenos Aires: Editorial Gillermo Kraft, 1942.

Cerisola, R. A. "Siluetas de detenidos-desaparecidos: Estética y política." In *Tomarte: Primer Encuentro Bienal Alternativo de Arte*. Rosario: 1990.

Elliot, David. *Art from Argentina*. Oxford: Museum of Modern Art, 1994.

Facio, Sara. *La fotografía en la Argentina: desde 1840 a nuestros días*. Buenos Aires: La Azotea, 1995.

———. "Fotografía: La memoria cuestionada." *Cuadernos hispano-americanos* 517–519 (1993): 269–79.

Foster, David William. "Sara Facio." *Buenos Aires: City and Culture*. Gainesville: University of Florida Press, forthcoming.

Gradowczyk, Mario. *Image and Memory; Photography from Latin America, 1866–1994*. Ed. Wendy Watriss and Lois Parkinson Zamora. Essays by Boris Kossoy and Fernando Castro. Austin: University of Texas Press, 1998.

King, John. *El Di Tella y el desarrollo cultural argentino en la década del sesenta*. Buenos Aires: Arte Gaglianone, 1985.

Molina, Enrique, and Angel Bonomini. *Molina Campos*. Buenos Aires: Asociación Amigos de las Artes Tradicionales, 1992.

Ortiz Monasterio, Pablo, ed. *Democracia vigilada: fotógrafos argentinos.* Prólogo de Miguel Bonasso. Mexico, D.F.: Fondo de Cultura Económica, 1988.

Premios Colección Costantini: 68 artistas 25 críticos. Buenos Aires: Museo Nacional de Bellas Artes, 1997.

Troche, Michel, and G. Gassiot-Talabot. *Berni.* Paris: Bibli Opus, 1971.

20 (veinte) obras maestras: arte argentino del siglo XX. Buenos Aires: Museo Nacional de Arte Decorativo/Banco Velox, 1996.

Index

ABOUT THE AUTHORS

DAVID WILLIAM FOSTER is Chair of the Department of Languages and Literatures and Regents' Professor of Spanish, Humanities, and Women's Studies at Arizona State University. He is the author of *Latin American Writers on Gay and Lesbian Themes: A Bio-Critical Sourcebook* (Greenwood, 1994).

MELISSA FITCH LOCKHART is on the faculty at Arizona International College of the University of Arizona in Tucson. She has published several articles on gender and sexuality in Latin American theatre and is currently writing a book on Latin American women writers.

DARRELL B. LOCKHART is a lecturer in Spanish at the University of Arizona. He is the editor of *Jewish Writers of Latin America: A Dictionary* (1997) and is the author of a forthcoming book, *Latin American Jewish Literature*, as well as the editor of a forthcoming collection of essays on Mexican Jewish Literature.